D1595333

Fundamentals of
Comparative Cognition

....

Fundamentals of Comparative Cognition

....

SARA J. SHETTLEWORTH

University of Toronto

New York   Oxford

OXFORD UNIVERSITY PRESS

Oxford University Press, Inc., publishes works that further Oxford University's
objective of excellence in research, scholarship, and education.

Oxford New York
Auckland   Cape Town   Dar es Salaam   Hong Kong   Karachi
Kuala Lumpur   Madrid   Melbourne   Mexico City   Nairobi
New Delhi   Shanghai   Taipei   Toronto

With offices in
Argentina   Austria   Brazil   Chile   Czech Republic   France   Greece
Guatemala   Hungary   Italy   Japan   Poland   Portugal   Singapore
South Korea   Switzerland   Thailand   Turkey   Ukraine   Vietnam

For titles covered by Section 112 of the US Higher Education Opportunity Act,
please visit www.oup.com/us/he for the latest information about
pricing and alternate formats.

Published by Oxford University Press, Inc.
198 Madison Avenue, New York, New York 10016
http://www.oup.com

Oxford is a registered trademark of Oxford University Press

Library of Congress Cataloging-in-Publication Data
Shettleworth, Sara J.
Fundamentals of comparative cognition / Sara J. Shettleworth, Paul Bloom,
    Lynn Nadel.—1st ed.
p. cm.—(The fundamentals of cognition series ; 2)
Includes bibliographical references and index.
ISBN 978-0-19-534310-6
1. Cognition.   2. Psychology, Comparative.   I. Bloom, Paul, 1963–
II. Nadel, Lynn.   III. Title.
BF311.S547 2013
153—dc23   2012000398

Printing number: 9 8 7 6 5 4 3 2 1

Printed in the United States of America
on acid-free paper

BRIEF CONTENTS

CONTENTS

....

SERIES INTRODUCTION

....

We conceived of the Fundamentals of Cognition series in recognition of an important need: when one teaches an advanced undergraduate course or an introductory graduate seminar, there frequently is no suitable book available. Based on our own experience and discussions with our colleagues, we feel the field needs a series of concise treatments of the fundamentals—primers. These provide state-of-the-art summaries while leaving ample room for additional reading of current material of the instructor's choice.

With this ideal in mind, each book in the Fundamentals of Cognition series has the following in common:

- It is concise.
- It is written by a leading scholar in the field, one who has also exhibited an ability to write about complex subjects in an accessible style.
- It provides a well-organized and up-to-date survey of our current understanding of major theories in the discipline.

We, in partnership with Oxford University Press, present the Fundamentals of Cognition.

Paul Bloom
Yale University
Lynn Nadel
University of Arizona

PREFACE
....

The comparative study of cognition is the area of the cognitive sciences most richly connected to the rest of behavioral biology, embracing not only every aspect of cognition but its development and evolution in all species, humans included. Research in comparative cognition also provides "animal models" for behavioral neuroscience and genetics and insights into the behavior of species we wish to conserve and protect. At its core, it asks what our minds share with those of the other creatures on this planet and what makes us unique.

Fundamentals of Comparative Cognition is a short text designed to convey the essence of this rich and exciting field. Like my monograph *Cognition, Evolution, and Behavior* (Shettleworth, 2010a), this book integrates research from laboratory and field, psychology and behavioral ecology/ethology. The *Fundamentals* especially emphasizes psychological principles, highlighting theoretical issues and experimental approaches that cut across specific research questions. It gives special attention to species comparisons, emphasizing sound evolutionary thinking and methods for testing comparative hypotheses about cognition. It includes the established foundations of the field along with new and controversial topics, such as whether any other animals plan or have theory of mind. Suggestions for Further Reading at the end of each chapter direct readers to more depth and detail. The book can thus serve as an up-to-date text for an undergraduate course or as the backbone of an advanced seminar or graduate course in comparative cognition. The material would also be appropriate for a component of a course in animal behavior, behavioral ecology, cognitive science, or behavioral neuroscience.

The organization reflects the current state of the field, with equal emphasis on basic processes, physical cognition, and social cognition. A short introductory chapter provides historical background and discusses key foundational issues such as approaches to species comparison and the roles of anthropomorphism and Lloyd Morgan's Canon, illustrated with examples from contemporary research. The three central chapters present the experimental approaches, data, and key theories. Basic Processes (Chapter 2) covers domain-general processes of perception, memory, associative learning, and category and concept learning. Physical Cognition (Chapter 3) includes space, time, number, instrumental behavior, foraging and economic decision making, and tool use. Social Cognition (Chapter 4) includes cognitive requirements of sociality, social learning and imitation, cooperation, theory of mind, and animal communication and its relationship to human language. Chapter 5 sums up by considering contemporary discussions of Darwin's claim that the human mind is "different in degree but not in kind" from that of other animals.

I thank Lynn Nadel and Paul Bloom for inviting me to contribute to this Oxford series, Patrick Lynch and Jane Potter at Oxford as well as the anonymous reviewers of the long-ago prospectus for encouragement and enthusiasm, and Lynn Nadel and Lynn Hasher for comments on specific chapters. Thanks to Amanda Seed, Roger Thompson, and Clive Wynne for thoughtfully and thoroughly reviewing the manuscript for Oxford; although I didn't agree with all their suggestions, they have undoubtedly helped make the book more accessible. Finally, once again I have the pleasure of thanking Margaret C. Nelson for her lovely illustrations. With all this expert help on text and figures, readers have only the author to blame for anything that remains unclear or misleading.

Sara J. Shettleworth
Toronto, September 2011

Fundamentals of
Comparative Cognition

....

CHAPTER 1

....

What Is Comparative Cognition About?

Comparative cognition is the study of cognitive processes in all species of animals, humans included. In this book, *cognition* embraces all processes involved in acquiring, storing, and using information from the environment, from perception to decision making, from a mouse's memory for familiar odors to a chimpanzee's apparently planful use of tools. The term *comparative* implies explicit comparisons of two or more species, but much comparative cognition research might be called the study of *animal cognition* because it focuses on just one non-human species or another. The goal of such research may be to compare the findings to those known from humans or to understand how particular species find their way around, choose food or mates, or the like. Either way, it contributes to the bigger picture of understanding the "endless minds most beautiful" (Finlay, 2007) of the other creatures on this planet, what they share and how they are unique, how and why they might have evolved.

From prehistoric times, interactions with other animals as prey, predators, or subjects of domestication have provided practical reasons for people to be interested in their minds and behavior. Practical considerations still motivate some research on animal cognition, such as that addressing issues in conservation and animal welfare. For instance, on some views how we treat animals in captivity should be determined by how closely their cognitive abilities resemble ours (see Dawkins, 2006). And much contemporary animal cognition research has the practical goal of developing "animal models" of human cognitive processes for use in investigating their neurobiological or genetic basis. This approach has

2 FUNDAMENTALS OF COMPARATIVE COGNITION

been especially successful in the study of memory (Chapter 2). But an equally important impetus for studying comparative cognition is sheer scientific curiosity. How *do* wood thrushes find their way from Pennsylvania to Central America in the fall and back again the next spring to the very same territory they occupied the year before? What does a baboon know about the complex social relationships among the other members of her troop, and how did she come to know it? What does her understanding of her social companions have in common with our understanding of our fellow human beings?

As the foregoing examples suggest, contemporary research on comparative cognition is multidisciplinary, with contributions not only from experimental psychologists but from biologists working in both laboratory and field, anthropologists, neurobiologists, and philosophers, among others. This makes for a lively and multifaceted research enterprise but also for the kinds of debate and disagreement that inevitably arise when people with different backgrounds and approaches try to communicate with one another. What unifies this diverse field is the overarching question with which the modern study of comparative cognition began, how true is Darwin's (1871) assertion that humans' "mental powers" are "different in degree but not in kind" from those of other species? For the first century or so after Darwin, students of comparative cognition were primarily concerned with documenting shared "mental powers," that is, cognitive processes, by looking for similarities between other animals and humans and by developing species-general theories of animal learning, memory, categorization, spatial representation, and the like. More recently the explosion of research on natural social groups of monkeys, apes, and other species has increased interest in social cognitive processes such as those involved in social learning and communication. Information from all these quarters has prompted reevaluation of Darwin's claim: although other species share many cognitive processes with us, a few may be uniquely human.

"From Darwin to Behaviorism": A Little History

In *The Origin of Species*, Darwin (1859) largely steered clear of the touchy topic of human evolution, but it was front and center in *The Descent of Man and Selection in Relation to Sex* (Darwin, 1871). The physical similarities between humans and apes might persuade some that they had evolved from a common ancestor, but evidence of mental similarity would be far more convincing. Accordingly, Chapters 2 and 3 of *The Descent of Man* marshaled evidence to show "… that there is no fundamental difference between man and the higher mammals in their mental faculties" (Darwin, 1871, p. 35). Darwin claimed that other animals share with humans memory, attention, imitation, reasoning, even imagination and aesthetic and moral sensibility. His primary evidence was *anecdotal*, that is, opportunistic observations made by him or reported by others that seemed consistent with some "mental power" or another. For instance, the fact that his dog came out of the barn and greeted Darwin when he arrived home from his five-year voyage on the *Beagle* was evidence that animals have very good memory. Although some of Darwin's arguments were more speculative, he recognized that we cannot easily draw conclusions about conscious processes such as abstraction and self-consciousness in animals. "This difficulty arises from the impossibility of judging what passes through the mind of an animal; and again the fact that writers differ to a great extent in the meaning which they attribute to … terms" (Darwin, 1879/2004, p. 105).

Darwin's writings inspired some of his supporters to seek further evidence for humanlike mental powers in nonhuman species. Primary among them was George Romanes (e.g. 1892), who could be less cautious than Darwin about interpreting anecdotes *anthropomorphically*, that is, by attributing humanlike behavior by an animal to humanlike thought and reasoning. For example, he suggested a cat that learned to open a gate must have seen people do it and reasoned, "If a hand can do it, why not a paw?" But such interpretations demand experimental tests, and around the beginning of the twentieth century relevant experiments began to appear, especially in the work of the American psychologist E. L. Thorndike (1911/1970). He placed cats and chicks in "puzzle boxes" from which they could escape by pulling strings, pushing levers, or the like. The animals showed no evidence of insightfully solving the problems but rather gradually became quicker to escape, learning by trial and error to perform the action that opened the box. Thorndike also found no evidence that any of the animals he tested could imitate a successful action performed by others of their species. For example, in a maze with two routes to food, chicks did not always follow the route they had seen a trained chick take.

The logic of Thorndike's simple test of imitation is fundamental to research on animal cognition (Heyes, 2008). Anthropomorphic interpretation of anecdotes like Romanes's story of the cat, that is, *folk psychology* (our everyday intuitive understanding of human psychology), suggests that animals should learn by copying others. But no matter how plausible the proposed explanation of a single observation or set of observations, there are nearly always other equally plausible explanations. In this case,

Thorndike's puzzle box data show that animals can learn gradually from the results of their own actions. The key then is to devise a situation in which the alternatives predict different outcomes. Here if chicks can imitate, the majority of them should follow the same route as the trained chick, whereas if they do not imitate in this situation but must learn where to go by individual trial and error, naive chicks will select the routes about 50:50 at first and about half of them will end up preferring each one. Unlike with purveying anecdotes, the goal of experiments such as these is not just to confirm that animals are (or are not) capable of doing something "clever" but to discover *how* they do what they do.

In experimental psychology, anthropomorphic interpretation of animal behavior along with the study of human subjective experience was largely eclipsed during the first two-thirds of the twentieth century by the development of behaviorism, which focused on observable behavior and eschewed explanation in terms of cognitive or other internal factors (Boakes, 1984). In research with animals, this approach reached its apotheosis with the work of B.F. Skinner and his followers, who studied the control of behavior by factors in the environment such as the stimuli present and the past schedule of reinforcement (reward and punishment). At more or less the same time in Europe, Konrad Lorenz, Niko Tinbergen, and their students, influenced by the Americans Craig and Whitman (see Burkhardt, 2005), developed the biological science of animal behavior, *ethology*. Ethology was distinct from psychology in that it embraced natural behavior of all kinds of animals. Ethologists worked primarily in the field studying behaviors such as mating, parenting, or foraging in insects, fish, and birds. But the ethologists' approach to behavior was as scrupulously objective as that of the Skinnerians. "Causal analysis" of behavior meant defining the current external stimuli and internal motivational conditions that, for example, caused a herring gull to roll an egg into its nest or a male stickleback fish to display courtship movements to a female (Burkhardt, 2005). But such analysis of *proximal* (i.e., immediate) *causes* was recognized as addressing only one of four questions that could be asked about behavior (Tinbergen, 1963). "Tinbergen's four questions" also include "How does behavior develop in the individual?" "How does it function in the animal's life, for example, in getting mates or reducing predation?" and "How did it evolve?" Although these questions are distinct, in ethology a complete understanding of any behavior includes answers to all of them (see Bolhuis & Verhulst, 2009).

The rigorous descriptions of behavior and relevant environmental stimuli characteristic of ethology and behaviorist psychology remain essential tools, but the latter part of the twentieth century saw major changes in the central theoretical questions about animal behavior being asked by both psychologists and biologists. In the early 1970s in experimental psychology, the success of the "cognitive revolution" in the study of human minds stimulated parallel studies of animal cognition (e.g., Hulse, Fowler, & Honig, 1978). Often this meant studying familiar laboratory animals such as rats and pigeons in familiar learning tasks, but now behavior was not the object of study in itself but a window into internal, cognitive processes such as memory and representation. For instance, a well-known phenomenon from Skinnerian studies was the "scalloped" pattern of responding on fixed-interval (FI) schedules of reinforcement. When reward is given at regular intervals of time for, say, pecking or pressing a lever, animals perform the rewarded response very little immediately after each reward but more and more as the time for the next reward approaches. To someone interested in deducing cognitive processes underlying behavior, scalloping suggests the animal is not simply responding for as long as it takes to get food but timing the intervals between feedings. This intuition is supported by the observation that when food is occasionally withheld, responding declines in a predictable way after the usual time of food delivery. Models of the internal clock or interval timing mechanism were proposed and tested by, for example, varying the interval to be timed and measuring how precisely different durations could be discriminated (Chapter 3).

Meanwhile the biological study of animal behavior was seeing the development of *behavioral ecology*, which uses mathematical models to address Tinbergen's questions about evolution and current function. Such models are based on the assumption that behavior will evolve which increases *fitness*, the representation of the individual's genes in the next generation. Thus, it should optimize achievement of short-term goals that contribute to fitness such as rate of food intake or encounter with mates. Behavioral ecologists' models of optimal behavior during foraging and other activities were initially developed and tested without much regard for the cognitive or other proximal mechanisms necessary for their predictions to be fulfilled. This approach was and continues to be very successful (Westneat & Fox, 2010), but it soon became apparent that deviations from functional predictions could often be understood in terms of cognitive constraints. For example, modeling the best "patch" of the environment to forage in involves taking into account the amount of energy provided by the food items in each patch, how long it takes to find each one, and the time required to travel between patches. Animals seem to need a great deal of precise information for behavior to fit the model perfectly, but they do not always have it. Perception of item quality inevitably has some error, learning may be incomplete, and memory is not always accurate. Such considerations, combined with the fact that tests of optimality models often had much in common with psychological studies of learning and choice, led to a more balanced approach, sometimes referred to as *cognitive ecology* (Dukas & Ratcliffe, 2009), in which studies of cognitive mechanisms are integrated with functional and evolutionary considerations, as discussed further in Chapter 3.

In the 1970s the biological study of animal behavior also saw the development of *cognitive ethology* in the writings of the distinguished biologist Donald Griffin (1978). Flying in the face of Tinbergen's (1951) injunctions against studying the unobservable processes of animal consciousness, Griffin claimed that the behaviorist approach denies important facts about animal behavior which ethologists should be trying to discover. He proposed frankly anthropomorphic explanations of all sorts of behaviors of all sorts of animals in terms of conscious thought and reasoning. For example, when a honeybee returns from a successful foraging trip and dances in the hive, she may be aware that she is telling other bees where the food is and want them to find it. As we see in Chapter 4, such questions have guided some important research on animal communication, but the results are not usually interpreted in terms of conscious awareness. Moreover, although Griffin's suggestions conflate the study of cognition with the study of consciousness, these are not necessarily the same. In everyday language we distinguish between merely responding to events and being conscious of them. Here *consciousness* refers to perceptual awareness, which can be distinguished from reflective consciousness, as might be shown in making a plan or deciding how well one knows the material for tomorrow's exam. Most people who study animal behavior, and others as well, would probably agree that animals have some form of perceptual awareness, but many question their possession of reflective or self-reflective consciousness (Dawkins, 2006). A related issue discussed in Chapter 5, but without implications for consciousness, is whether animals are capable of only first-order representations of events or whether some have higher order representations (Penn, Holyoak, & Povinelli, 2008). First-order representations are based on purely perceptual features of events, such as "he is making a fist" or "the tomato is red." Second-order representations involve abstractions from first-order properties: "he *feels angry*" or "the tomato is *the same color as* the strawberry."

In any case, most contemporary students of comparative cognition eschew discussion of the tricky subject of animal consciousness. Processes such as memory and attention are defined in terms of observable behaviors, what the animal does, not how it feels while doing it. This is true even when tackling questions suggested by our own introspection, such as bees' understanding of other bees' need to know. Pinning down humanlike cognitive processes in other animals means looking for *functional similarity* of behaviors across species. As a simple example, we might test a person's recognition memory by asking her, "Did you see this word earlier?" whereas we might test a mouse's recognition memory by training it to choose the one odor out of two that it encountered more recently. We could then vary factors known to affect human memory to see whether the mouse's performance changes as expected for a measure of memory. For instance, the longer the time since exposure to the to-be-remembered odor, the fewer correct choices the mouse should make. In the more challenging investigation of Griffin's suggestion about the bees, we would need to specify what behavior is evidence of sensitivity to another bee's need to know. The logic of functional similarity is a basic tool in comparative cognition research (Heyes, 2008), even though, as in the case of the honeybees, deciding what constitutes functional similarity between observable animal behavior and evidence of some interesting human cognitive process is not always straightforward or uncontroversial.

Research in the Twenty-First Century: Tool-Using Crows

An instructive example of contemporary research integrating the multiple approaches to comparative cognition is the study of tool use by New Caledonian crows. New Caledonian crows are a species of corvid (the bird family that also includes ravens, jays, and nutcrackers) found on the islands of the New Caledonian archipelago, a thousand miles or so east of Australia. Several populations of these crows use sticklike tools during foraging, mainly to extract prey from logs and crevices (Fig. 1.1). They make some of the tools they use, among other ways by nibbling off the stiff ribs of *Pandanus* palm leaves and shaping the edge into hook- or wedge-like structures (Bluff, Weir, Rutz, Wimpenny, & Kacelnik, 2007; Hunt, 1996). The shapes of tools differ in different parts of New Caledonia, suggesting that specific tool-making techniques are transmitted socially from one generation to another, making crow tool manufacture a candidate for animal culture (Holzhaider, Hunt, & Gray, 2010).

FIGURE 1.1. New Caledonian crows using stick tools. After a video frame with permission of Gavin Hunt and the University of Aukland.

Tool use by any animal attracts attention because this skill has traditionally been thought to be uniquely human, or at least the privilege of species such as chimpanzees that are closely related to humans. However, it turns out that animals from many widely separated branches of the evolutionary tree use tools (Chapter 3 and Bentley-Condit & Smith, 2010). Even among primates, tool use is not entirely predicted by relatedness to humans (Fig. 1.2). For example, the most widespread use of the greatest variety of tools is documented for chimpanzees, but bonobos (about as closely related to humans) do not seem to use tools very much in the wild, whereas orangutans (less closely related) do. Because birds are not closely related to humans, the apparently routine use and manufacture of tools by New Caledonian crows is even more compelling evidence that some special ecological conditions rather than a humanlike brain are key to evolution of tool use. What these conditions might be is suggested by the only other similar bird tool user, the woodpecker finch of the Galapagos Islands. Woodpecker finches use twigs and cactus spines to extract food from holes and crevices. They are not corvids nor their especially close relatives, but like New Caledonian crows they evolved on islands with no competing species such as woodpeckers that could harvest the same resources more efficiently.

In terms of evolutionary biology, tool use by chimpanzees and other apes is shared with human tool use by *homology*, or descent from a comparatively recent common ancestor that is assumed to have been a tool

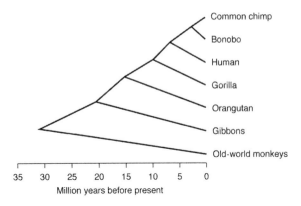

FIGURE **1.2.** Evolutionary relatedness (phylogenetic tree) of the four great ape species, humans, gibbons (lesser apes), and old-world monkeys. Further explanation in the text. Adapted from Ernard & Pääbo (2004) with permission.

user. Similarity in species' DNA and known rates of random mutation are used to make inferences about evolutionary relatedness, as illustrated in Figure 1.2 by the *phylogenetic* (or evolutionary) *tree* for humans, great apes (chimpanzees, bonobos, gorillas, and orangutans), lesser apes (gibbons), and old-world monkeys. The nodes (points at sharp angles) show when, in million years before the present, groups or individual species diverged from inferred common ancestors. For example, the last ancestor bonobos and chimpanzees have in common with humans is thought to have lived about six million years ago. All three species have evolved since then from an unknown common ancestor that was neither a chimpanzee nor a modern human. Chimpanzees and bonobos began to evolve as distinct species even more recently. Because the last ancestor shared by birds and primates was some much more ancient primitive vertebrate that presumably did not use tools, bird tool use represents separate or *convergent* evolution in unrelated species as a consequence of common ecological conditions. The crows' tool use is *analogous* to human tool use, whereas that of apes is *homologous*. This distinction matters for discussions of cognitive evolution because analogous behaviors are probably less likely than homologous ones to be mediated by the same mechanisms.

Of course, tool use was thought to be uniquely human (or at least uniquely primate) in the first place because it seems to reflect high intelligence—inventiveness, understanding of physical principles, a large brain, perhaps the ability to teach complex skills to others and to learn from them. But there are a number of problems with this anthropomorphic assumption, beginning with the idea of intelligence itself as applied to animals. Most people think they know what they mean by *intelligence* in everyday language; such an understanding is part of our folk psychology. But surprisingly often animal behaviors that appear intelligent at first glance turn out to be the product of remarkably "stupid" mechanisms (Shettleworth, 2010b). For example, a desert ant wandering out from its nest in search of food runs straight back home even from hundreds of meters away once it finds a prey item (Fig. 3.1c in Chapter 3). The ant looks as if it knows exactly where its home is, but in fact it knows only what distance and direction it needs to travel to get there. Place the ant with its food down somewhere else before the homeward trip and it runs in the same direction and for the same distance, then starts circling around as if expecting to find the nest. An ant wandering across the featureless desert has little spatial information other than distances and directions. It encodes these with great precision (Chapter 3), but the simple experiment just described reveals that it uses only the information it needs under normal conditions. Whether we want to describe it as intelligent or not is beside the point when it comes to analyzing the mechanisms underlying its behavior. We might want to say that "intelligence" is behavior that promotes survival and reproduction, that is, fitness, in natural conditions for the species, but this would render the term almost meaningless. We might also note that a person trying to perform like the ant on an appropriate relative spatial scale might fail miserably.

Besides highlighting the *anthropocentrism* (i.e., human-centeredness) in applying *intelligence* to animal behavior, the homing of the desert ant underlines a second point: *intelligence* in humans implies the general overall ability supposedly measured by IQ tests, whereas cognition in animals (and to some extent in humans) is *modular*. *Modularity*, the property of being made up of somewhat self-contained and independently functioning parts, is almost the rule when it comes to biological structures, but in the cognitive sciences the suggestion that human cognition is modular has been surprisingly controversial (see Barrett & Kurzban, 2006). However, other species provide plenty of evidence for a modular organization of cognition, with distinct abilities for distinct domains of information that have distinct abstract computational requirements. The desert ant is a superb navigator, but it doesn't use tools. It computes the distance it travels over the ground by implicitly counting steps (Wittlinger, Wehner, & Wolf, 2007), but it probably cannot enumerate arbitrary items as monkeys do

(Chapter 3). As another example, Clark's nutcrackers store thousands of pine seeds for the winter and have the excellent spatial memory required for retrieving them, but in laboratory tasks nutcrackers remember colors no better than other corvids and are worse than more social corvids at remembering the locations of items they saw other birds store (Balda & Kamil, 2006). That is, desert ants or Clark's nutcrackers are not exceptionally "intelligent" in general, just especially good at specific skills that are important for their survival and reproduction.

The nutcracker's exceptional spatial memory is an example of an *adaptive specialization* of cognition, an ability (spatial memory) shared across species but tweaked in each one in a way appropriate to its way of life. Physical structures and sensory systems (Chapter 2) provide many examples of adaptive specialization of shared characters. For instance, all birds have beaks but their shapes vary according to how they feed— tearing meat, cracking seeds, digging for worms, probing for nectar, and so on. Specific beak shapes are referred to as *adaptive* because they are assumed to have evolved as individuals with approximations to them experienced increased fitness compared to *conspecifics* (others of the same species) with other kinds of beaks. Of course, specialized structures are often accompanied by specializations in behavior and cognition. For instance, a hawk-like beak goes along with excellent stereoscopic vision and the ability to catch fast-moving prey. Cognitive adaptations would be expected to be reflected in neural specializations. An example in food-storing birds such as nutcrackers is correlation of the size of the hippocampus, a structure important for spatial memory in birds and mammals, with dependence on storing and retrieving food (Sherry, 2006).

It is rarely possible to prove hypotheses about adaptations because evolution proceeds so slowly, but evolutionary biologists have several kinds of evidence for them. These include comparing closely related species to see whether they differ in ways appropriate to differences in the environments they inhabit and observing how well present-day structures and behaviors work. The fact that animal species differ in cognitive specializations supports a modular analysis of cognition. But modular organization need not preclude some processes common to or cutting across domains (Barrett & Kurzban, 2006; Jeffery, 2010; West-Eberhard, 2003). These include perception, memory, and the simple forms of learning discussed in Chapter 2. In any case, evidence for modularity in animal cognition undermines the assumption that animals have some sort of general intelligence analogous to human IQ (but see Matzel & Kolata, 2010).

Returning to the New Caledonian crows, folk psychology suggests that when we call an animal tool-user intelligent we mean the animal understands what it is doing or knows how the tool works. New Caledonian crows certainly look as if they are doing more than performing a learned behavior describable as "insert a stick, wiggle it around, pull out a grub." Understanding tools implies the ability to use them flexibly as the situation requires. This assumption has led to a variety of tests of what tool-using animals understand (Chapter 3). In one used first with monkeys, the animal can get a piece of food out of a long transparent horizontal tube by pushing or pulling on it with a stick. Once animals are proficient at this task, a "trap" is introduced in the middle of the tube: food directed toward it falls in and is lost (see Fig. 3.7 in Chapter 3). An animal that understands what the stick tool is doing has to notice the location of the food relative to the trap and insert the stick so as to move the food away from it. "Understanding" suggests animals should choose the correct end right away. Instead, however, all animals tested so far, both birds and primates, choose randomly at first and learn to choose correctly—sometimes surprisingly slowly—indicating that trial and error is required.

The trap tube test opposes anthropomorphic predictions to an alternative, here trial-and-error learning. The theoretical bias in the field of comparative cognition is very strongly toward explaining behavior in terms of such basic species-general mechanisms rather than invoking processes like reasoning or understanding. This bias is the expression of a principle known as *Lloyd Morgan's Canon*, stated by the early comparative psychologist Conwy Lloyd Morgan (1894, p. 53): "In no case may we interpret an action as the outcome of the exercise of a higher psychical faculty, if it can be interpreted as the outcome of the exercise of one which stands lower in the psychological scale."

The Canon has plenty of problems (Sober, 2005). For instance, how do we judge "high" and "low"? The assumption that there is a "psychological scale" seems to reflect belief in a single *phylogenetic scale* of species, in which, for example, primates are more highly evolved than rats, which are higher than birds, which are higher than fish, which are higher than worms, and so on. The phylogenetic scale erroneously assumes linear progress in evolution rather than a Darwinian branching tree like that in Figure 1.2. A reasonable modern interpretation of Morgan's Canon is that explanations in terms of general processes of learning along with species-typical perceptual and response biases should always be sought before invoking more complex or specialized cognitive processes. This stance is justified by the fact that the simple forms of learning such as habituation and classical conditioning discussed in Chapter 2 are very widespread in the animal kingdom, having been found in all species tested, including fruit flies and nematode worms (Papini, 2008). They may reflect ancient adaptations of neural circuits to universal causal regularities in the world. Because it is a good bet that any new species we study shares the capability for these forms of learning, the burden of proof is on anyone proposing that some novel, additional, cognitive mechanism has arisen on a particular branch of the evolutionary tree.

As for the New Caledonian crows, one might ask, if their tool using behavior is the result of trial-and-error learning, why don't more species of birds regularly use tools? The "why" in this question has answers in each of Tinbergen's four senses. We have seen a hint of the answer to the evolutionary "why" in special conditions on islands. The functional "why" could be addressed by determining the importance of foods obtained with tools in the crows' diet in the field (see Bluff et al., 2007). And as we have seen, tests of the underlying cognitive mechanisms suggest that the proximate causes do not include a specialized kind of physical understanding and therefore may be shared by many species. That leaves the question of how tool use develops, a question addressed by hatching and raising four New Caledonian crows in a lab in Oxford (Bluff et al., 2007). To test the notion that tool use was learned by observing older animals, two of the young crows had a keeper who demonstrated tool use in a controlled way, extracting food from crevices with sticks while the little crows watched. The other two were not allowed to see people or other crows using tools. Nevertheless, all four animals began to pick up sticks and poke them into holes at about the same age, and all were soon using them to obtain food. Thus, what is apparently special about the crows—and woodpecker finches as well (see Bluff et al., 2007)—is not their possession of some special tool-related cognitive ability but the tendency to perform early precursors to tool use. These get trial-and-error learning started, although interactions with tool-using adults also play a role (Bluff, Troscianko, Weir, Kacelnik, & Rutz, 2010; Holzhaider et al., 2010).

This study of how tool use develops makes a final important general point: attempting to classify behavior as *learned* as opposed to *innate* is meaningless. Trial-and-error learning likely perfects the crows' skill, but it operates on appropriate motor patterns which they are predisposed to engage in. By the same token, tool use is not innate either, if by *innate* we mean performed without any relevant experience. And if we mean by *innate* not modifiable by experience once it is performed, that cannot be correct either. Every moment of an organism's development from the very beginning results from a seamless interplay of the learned and the innate, or genes and environment. Genes determine how the environment influences development and subsequent behavior, and the reverse. Nothing in behavior or cognition is either wholly learned or entirely innate. Even species-specific abilities such as bird's singing a certain kind of song are the product of both the individual's species-typical genes and a species-typical developmental trajectory, including contact with singing adults of its species. Thus, as with *intelligent*, classifying behavior as innate or genetically determined versus learned or environmentally determined is meaningless, if indeed it ever made sense outside of folk psychology (Bateson & Mameli, 2007).

Two major approaches to research in comparative cognition converge in the studies of tool use by New Caledonian crows, the traditional psychological or anthropocentric approach on the one hand and the ecological or biological approach on the other. The one tradition focuses on studying cognitive processes in animals (here those underlying tool use) as they may illuminate or resemble processes in humans, whereas the other addresses cognitive mechanisms underlying ecologically relevant behavior in nature and does so in the context of Tinbergen's questions about evolution, function, proximal causation, and development. In the rest of the book we will often be looking at the psychological building blocks of such synthetic research, for example, the effects of reward or the characteristics of memory, based on studies of a few species in the laboratory. But there will also be further examples of ways in which such findings are enriched, challenged, and extended by integrating information from other areas of behavioral biology. In the early twenty-first century anthropocentrism means thinking about the phylogeny and evolution of human cognitive capacities: which are shared with other species by common descent or convergence and which are unique to humans and why. These questions are the focus of Chapter 5.

How This Book Is Organized

This book takes a "bottom-up" approach to comparative cognition, going from basic domain-general processes shared across vertebrates and many invertebrates and building up to apparently more complex domain-specific processes such as social understanding and language.

Thus, it traces Darwin's argument from the processes most widely shared to those possibly unique to humans. This organization also reflects the development of much comparative cognition research within experimental psychology by starting, in Chapter 2, with the processes that have been studied the longest and hence are best understood: animal perception, memory, habituation or learning about single events, associative learning (classical and instrumental conditioning), discrimination, and category learning. With this foundation we can better appreciate the specialized or modular aspects of the processes for dealing with specific domains of physical and social information. Chapter 3 looks at processes specific to acquiring, storing, and acting on information about the physical world: space, time, number, tools and the consequences of action. In Chapter 4 we look at processes specific to individuals' interactions with one another: social learning, imitation, understanding of others' goals and intentions, and communication. Chapter 5 integrates material from the rest of the book by revisiting Darwin's claim that humans differ mentally from other species only in degree, not in kind. We will see that the recent explosion of comparative research has given reason to question Darwin's claim and provided grounds for proposing some quite specific ways in which human cognition is unique as well as yielding new evidence for sophisticated nonverbal processes that we share with other species.

Suggestions for Further Reading

These are mainly books with further depth and detail on the approaches to animal cognition and behavior introduced in this chapter. The Web sites of the Comparative Cognition Society and the Animal Behavior Society are also recommended for links to news and Web sites of individual scientists, many of which have photo and video illustrations of their research.

Boakes, R. (1984). *From Darwin to Behaviourism*. Cambridge: Cambridge University Press.

Bolhuis, J., & Verhulst, S. (Eds.). (2009). *Tinbergen's Legacy: Function and Mechanism in Behavioral Biology*. Cambridge: Cambridge University Press.

Dukas, R., & Ratcliffe, J. M. (Eds.). (2009). *Cognitive Ecology II*. Chicago: The University of Chicago Press.

Heyes, C. (2008). Beast machines? Questions of animal consciousness. In M. Davies & L. Weiskrantz (Eds.), *Frontiers of Consciousness* (pp. 259–274). Oxford: Oxford University Press.

Papini, M. R. (2008). *Comparative Psychology* (2nd ed.). New York: Psychology Press.

Pearce, J. M. (2008). *Animal Learning & Cognition* (3rd ed.). New York: Psychology Press.

Shettleworth, S. J. (2010). *Cognition, Evolution, and Behavior* (2nd ed.). New York: Oxford University Press. Chapters 1 and 2.

Striedter, G. F. (2005). *Principles of Brain Evolution*. Sunderland, MA: Sinauer Associates.

Tinbergen, N. (1951). *The Study of Instinct*. Oxford: Oxford University Press.

Vonk, J., & Shackleford, T. (Eds.). (2012). *Oxford Handbook of Comparative Evolutionary Psychology*. New York: Oxford University Press.

Westneat, D. F., & Fox, C. W. (Eds.). (2010). *Evolutionary Behavioral Ecology*. New York: Oxford University Press.

CHAPTER 2

....

Basic Processes

The simplest behavior consists of reflexes, direct connections between sensory channels and response-generating mechanisms. But most behavior of interest in this book implies some more elaborate internal intervening structure or process. For instance, inputs from multiple sensory channels may be integrated into representations of objects and situations. The effects of sensory events may be retained, as evident in changed behavior toward later occurrences of the same events; that is, animals exhibit memory. And repeated encounters with the same temporal or spatial pattern of events may result in learning their relationship.

The basic processes of perception, memory, and learning characterized by these statements are found in all sorts of animals (Papini, 2008). They can be the building blocks of more complex processes such as learning categories and concepts, finding one's way around in space, and navigating complex social networks. Nowadays, applying Morgan's Canon (Chapter 1) often means trying to distinguish behavior based on such simple phylogenetically general cognitive processes from that based on apparently more complex or specialized ones. Indeed, for some authors, only the latter are meaningfully "cognitive" (see Shettleworth, 2010a). However, this book embraces all mechanisms involved in acquiring, storing, and acting on information from the environment, how they work, what distinguishes them from one another, and which species have them. Thus, we begin with basic mechanisms of perception, memory, and learning, and the job of this chapter is to convey them. Along the way we will encounter some important foundational issues. How can we compare cognition in different species? How can we study processes in animals that in humans are accompanied by distinctive subjective experiences? We begin with a brief look at how animals perceive the world.

Perception and Attention

Most animals sense the world very differently from the way humans do. A lasting contribution of the founders of ethology was von Uexküll's (1934/1957) concept of the *Umwelt*, or self-world, of animals. Understanding behavior begins with understanding the features of the world a species' sense organs can respond to and the things important to it, the species' *Umwelt*. Most important, some species sense physical energies imperceptible to unaided humans. The platypus feeds underwater at night with its eyes, ears, and nostrils closed, guided by the responses of sensors in its bill to the electric fields generated by movements of its prey. Bats find their way around and catch moths in the dark guided by echoes from their own ultrasonic vocalizations. Some birds navigate with information from the Earth's magnetic field by means which may include responses of cells in the visual system, in effect "seeing" compass directions.

Examples of exceptional sensory systems like these bring home the fact that other animals may live in worlds unimaginably different from ours. More subtle but equally important to bear in mind are ecologically relevant specializations of familiar sensory systems. For example, as might be expected of nocturnal animals, rats lack color vision and have poor visual acuity, but they have exquisite olfactory sensitivity (Whishaw & Kolb, 2005). Vision is more important to diurnal (day-active) animals, but they do not necessarily see the same things we do. Color vision in honeybees and birds is based on different distributions of wavelength sensitivity than in primates. Because the sensitivity of honeybees and some birds extends into the ultraviolet (UV), a researcher looking at a flower or a brightly colored male bird may not have an accurate picture of what a bee or a female bird is responding to (Briscoe & Chittka, 2001; Cuthill et al., 2000).

Often closely related species, or even different populations of the same species, differ adaptively in the signals they produce and/or in perceptual sensitivity. For instance, different sounds travel best in forests versus open meadows; the songs of birds from these two habitats differ accordingly. The study of how animal signals and responses to them are adapted to the environment is *sensory ecology* (Endler, Westcott, Madden, & Robson, 2005). Research in sensory ecology underlines the general principle that even basic characters that many species share, such as a visual or auditory system, tend to be specialized in each one to suit its own way of life. Such differences have important adaptive consequences. Later we consider whether this same kind of specialization applies to learning, memory, and other aspects of cognition.

Modifying methods for studying human perception and attention to test other species reveals that many of the same principles hold across the animal kingdom. (cf. Cook, 2001). For example, in studies of attention during visual search, subjects search for a *target* item among a field of more or less similar *distractors*. The target might be a letter *X* in a field of *O*s as on the left of Figure 2.1, or a black *X* in a field of black and white *X*s and *O*s (Fig. 2.1, right). People are told to find the target as quickly as possible, whereas animals are rewarded for indicating a distinctive item in some way, such as pecking it in the case of birds. Unlike humans, animals must be given their "instructions" through lengthy training. They might start with the target and a single distractor. The number of distractors would be increased gradually as accuracy improves. Just as with people, performance is better when the target differs from the distractors in only one feature (e.g., letter shape) than in multiple features (e.g., shape and color, a case of *conjunctive search*). Especially in conjunctive search, accuracy is lower and/or targets are detected more slowly as the number of distractors or their similarity to the target increases (Zentall, 2005).

In simple search tasks, such as finding an *X* among *O*s (Fig. 2.1), people report that the target seems to "pop out." The short latencies of other species under such conditions suggest the same is true for them (*latency* is the inverse of speed, so short latency means high speed). Conjunctive

FIGURE 2.1. Examples of stimuli for visual search experiments. (*Left*) A target defined by a difference in one feature (shape) "pops out." (*Right*) Conjunctive search. The same target takes longer to find when two features (here shape and color) must be attended to.

search requires focused attention; subjects behave as if comparing items to the target one at a time. With multiple possible targets, performance improves under conditions that in effect allow the subject to predict the next target. For instance, in a conjunctive search for black *X*s and white *O*s, detection of black *X*s improves after several black *X*s in succession or after a cue that the next target is a black *X* while detection of alternative targets is impaired. Here attention is said to be *primed*. Priming has been well documented in animals, especially pigeons and other birds (Blough, 2006). When animals are foraging in nature, priming of attention is manifested as a *search* (or *searching*) *image*. Encountering several items of the same type in succession improves detection of that type and degrades detection of others, as if the animal learns what to look for. Laboratory studies of search image have employed pigeons searching for grains mixed with multicolored gravel (Reid & Shettleworth, 1992) and blue jays searching for images of moths on images of tree trunks (Bond, 2007).

The flip side of focused attention is divided attention, classically described as "the cocktail party effect," after the difficulty of following more than one conversation at once in a crowded room. In other species, too, performance on one task falls when attention must be shared between it and another task (Zentall, 2005). In naturalistic situations, fish feed more slowly when watching for predators, and blue jays detect prey less efficiently when they appear in multiple "patches" on a computer screen rather than in one (Dukas & Kamil, 2000). Why attention should be limited is an interesting and unresolved theoretical question touching both mechanism and function; such examples indicate that the difficulty of attending to several things at once has a cost in nature (Dukas, 2004).

Memory

Elements of Animal Memory

Tap a snail's shell, and the animal withdraws into it. Tap whenever the snail extends its body again, and it gradually withdraws less and less. This is an example of *habituation*, perhaps the simplest form of memory, that is, retention of the effects of experience from one occasion to the next. Habituation can be distinguished from sensory fatigue by demonstrating *dishabituation*: brief presentation of a different stimulus restores the original response. For example, the *startle response* is a primitive defensive reflex of rats and other mammals to a sudden strong stimulus such

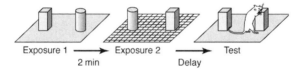

Exposure 1 ⟶ Exposure 2 ⟶ Test
2 min   Delay

FIGURE 2.2. Procedure for testing encoding of place, context, and identity during habituation. In each distinct "exposure" context, the two objects are arranged differently. Some time ("delay") after rats have explored them in each context, they encounter two copies of one object in one of the exposure contexts. Preferential investigation of the object that is in a new location for that context is evidence for episodic-like memory. After Eacott and Norman (2004) with permission.

as a loud noise. A rat crouches and draws its head and limbs close to its body. After startle to a noise begins to habituate, a brief flash of a novel light enhances startle to the next noise.

Confusingly, *dishabituation* is also used as a label for the restoration of an habituated response when a novel test stimulus similar to the habituating stimulus is presented. In effect, the animal reveals that it notices the difference between the test stimulus and the original. Figure 2.2 shows an example with rats' tendency to explore novel objects (Eacott & Norman, 2004). During exploration, rats learn not only features of an object itself but also the context (here, floor color) and location where they encounter it. The procedure is an example of the *habituation-dishabituation paradigm*, frequently used to discover what features of the world animals remember. Here the animals received no training or extraneous reward but revealed what they spontaneously stored in memory during a relatively brief experience.

Notice that memory is identified operationally, in terms of behavioral change, without reference to awareness, conscious recollection, or the like. This approach is consistent with most traditional research on human memory. Relatively recently, students of human memory have begun to study memory processes that are accompanied by distinct conscious states, often along with studies of associated brain processes. Later in this section we look at some studies with animals inspired by such work.

Although tests like that illustrated in Figure 2.2 provide a simple and elegant way to study memory, they can be used only with events that elicit clear untrained responses. Contemporary studies of animal memory

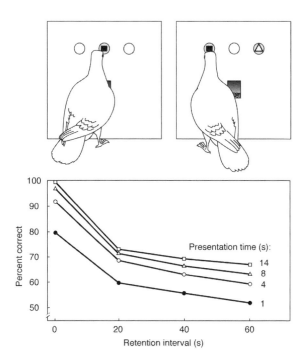

FIGURE 2.3. (*Top*) Delayed matching to sample procedure for pigeons. The sample appears on the center key and the pigeon pecks it (*left*). After the retention interval, sample and distractor appear on the side keys and the pigeon is reinforced (grain appears below the keys) for pecking the sample (*right*). Redrawn from Wright (1991) with permission. (*Bottom*) Effects of retention interval and sample presentation time on pigeons' matching to sample performance. Redrawn from Grant (1976) with permission.

more often involve some sort of training. One widely used task is *delayed matching to sample*, illustrated with pigeons in Figure 2.3. In the study phase of each trial, the animal is exposed to a to-be-remembered stimulus, the *sample*, here a pattern on a lighted disk that a bird pecks (a *pecking key*). Exposure to the sample is followed by a period during which the animal must hold it in memory, the *retention interval*. In the test of memory following the retention interval (Fig. 2.3, right), the sample reappears along with one or more other stimuli, the distractors, and the animal is rewarded if it chooses (here pecks) the sample. Reward or nonreward is followed by a rest between trials, the *intertrial interval* or *ITI*. Then the sequence of events begins again with the same or a different sample, typically in a random sequence.

The same terms as in the study of human memory are used to refer to the processes thought to be engaged at each stage of such a trial. Presentation of the sample results in *encoding* of the sample in memory. This is not necessarily a direct record of sensory activity (a stimulus trace) but a transformation of it. For example, under some conditions pigeons apparently encode the sample in terms of what they must do on the test (e.g., "peck the square," a *prospective code*). In any case, animals may not encode every feature of to-be-remembered items. Attention, among other factors, may influence encoding (Zentall, 2005). Whatever was encoded is said to be *stored* in memory for the duration of the retention interval and may be *retrieved* at the time of test. As in everyday language, loss of memory is *forgetting*. But performance in a test of memory may decline over time without much if any forgetting. For instance, when a signal such as a tone or a light has been paired with a reinforcer (or reward) such as food or a shock, presenting the reinforcer right before a test with the signal alone restores performance otherwise lost during the retention interval. The effect of such a *reminder treatment* is one example of how memory is best retrieved when the motivational, temporal, and physical context most resembles that of training (Bouton & Moody, 2004). Similarly, when animals learn first one thing and then another in the same situation, performance on the second task may decline as time passes due to *interference* from the conflicting memory of the first. Performance can be restored by removing the opportunity to make the first-learned, interfering response (Cheng & Wignall, 2006).

Delayed matching to sample and habituation are tests of *recognition memory*: during the test, the sample is presented again as a *retrieval cue*, and the animal's behavior indicates whether it has a memory of a past encounter with that stimulus. Tests of *recall* are also frequently used with human subjects: in the absence of a target event, people indicate what they remember about it. They are rare with other species (but see Basile & Hampton, 2011). Notice that in studies of recognition memory, animals are tested simply for remembering the identity of a stimulus, not for whether it was paired with food or the like. The latter would involve *associative memory* (or *learning*). In neurobiological and genetic studies, tests of associative learning and recognition memory alike are generally referred to as tests of memory.

Retention intervals in most laboratory studies of animal memory are fairly short, from seconds or minutes (as in Fig. 2.3) to a few hours or days at most. Studies of very long-term memory in animals are rare (but see Fagot & Cook, 2006). Delayed matching is a test of *working memory*, as opposed to *reference memory*. Unlike in discussions of human memory, working memory here refers to memory for the distinctive features of each trial, such as the identity of the sample. Reference memory is memory for the stable features of the task, such as the requirement to peck the sample. These terms apply regardless of the duration of the memories being tested. For instance, in the popular *radial maze* test of spatial memory, rats collect food from eight or more baited locations without revisiting sites already emptied. Already-visited sites are samples to be held in working memory until the end of the trial, which may be hours after the first few sites are visited.

Conditions during presentation of a sample, during the retention interval, and at test all affect recognition memory in animals much as they do in humans (see Wright, 2006). Performance is better the longer the sample duration and the shorter the retention interval (Fig. 2.3). Longer intertrial intervals also improve performance, by reducing interference between similar memories from successive trials. Reduction in interference also likely explains why monkeys' performance is improved by *trial-unique* samples, that is, samples presented only once per daily session. By the same token, repeated use of a few similar samples (e.g., two colors) probably helps to account for pigeons' relatively quick forgetting in typical delayed matching tasks. However, although qualitative features of memory such as those illustrated in Figure 2.3 are generally the same across species, species do differ in the kinds of events they best remember. To some extent this reflects differences in sensory abilities. For instance, pigeons have amazingly (to us) detailed and capacious visual memory (Cook, Levison, Gillett, & Blaisdell, 2005), whereas rats excel in olfactory and spatial memory (Slotnick, 2001). In addition, some researchers have hypothesized that closely related species facing different demands on memory in the wild differ adaptively in memory, but this idea can be difficult to test, as we see next.

Comparing Memory across Species

When people say that some animals are "smarter" than others, they sometimes mean animals differ in how much and how long they can remember. Tests of this idea date from the early days of experimental comparative psychology (Hunter, 1913). Nowadays it is generally accepted that firm conclusions about cognitive differences among species can be drawn only after extensive research that takes account of what MacPhail (e.g., 1987) called *contextual variables*, features of experimental procedures that might affect species differently. For example, to compare how long dogs and parrots remember where they saw food hidden, we should be sure the food has equal value for both species. Otherwise, differences in performance could arise because one species is more attentive to the baiting and/or motivated to obtain the food at test. One way to deal with such confounds is *systematic variation* (Bitterman, 1975; Papini, 2008) of the suspected contextual variables. Here this would mean varying the animals' hunger and/or the food to see whether motivation influenced whether dogs or parrots perform better. And of course features of the procedure such as how the to-be-remembered events are presented, the duration of the retention interval, and the number of distractors present at test should be the same for all the species being tested. But these are contextual variables, too, making the process of systematic variation potentially endless (Kamil, 1988). Nevertheless, the challenges of comparing cognitive processes in different species can be met. The rest of this section reviews two research programs that have done so, one with a group of closely related species and the other with very divergent ones.

The research of Kamil, Balda, and their colleagues with the food-storing corvids of the American Southwest (Balda & Kamil, 2006) has used multiple tests of abilities predicted to vary with ecology. The four birds they study—Clark's nutcrackers, pinyon jays, scrub jays, and Mexican jays—differ in the extent to which they store food in scattered locations and rely on their caches for sustenance throughout the winter. Clark's nutcrackers are caching specialists, storing thousands of caches of pine seeds in late summer and retrieving them even the next spring when feeding their young. Because retrieving so many caches from under the snow seems to demand precise and capacious memory for locations, nutcrackers should have exceptional spatial memory. This hypothesis has been tested in ways ranging from letting the birds store seeds in a large laboratory room and testing retrieval weeks or months later to training them on spatial delayed matching tasks similar to that in Figure 2.3. Although all four species can learn the tasks, nutcrackers generally perform most accurately. In contrast, with colors as samples in conventional delayed matching, the nutcrackers were no better than the other three species, indicating that their superiority in spatial tasks is not due to some contextual variable like adaptability to the lab or fondness for the rewards. The same four species differ in sociality in a way that predicts a different pattern of species differences in tasks tapping social cognitive skills. Pinyon jays and Mexican jays cache while in large flocks, whereas nutcrackers and scrub jays are comparatively solitary. Consistent with this observation, pinyon and Mexican jays remember locations of caches they saw other birds make as well as they remember their own caches, whereas nutcrackers do not (see Balda & Kamil, 2006).

The hypothesis that birds reliant on stored food have better spatial memory than related species that store less or not at all has also been tested with chickadees and tits (*parids*) with generally similar results (Shettleworth & Hampton, 1998). Even populations within a species that face more or less severe winters, such as black-capped chickadees in Alaska versus the lowlands of Colorado, can differ in spatial memory and size of the hippocampus, the brain area involved in spatial memory in mammals and birds (Roth & Pravosudov, 2009). The broader hypothesis that animals facing greater demands on spatial memory in the wild have both better spatial memory and an enlargement of the hippocampus relative to the rest of the brain has also been tested by comparing birds from a given species that migrate to different extents, rodents that have different sized territories, and birds that use memory to different extents in finding places to lay their eggs (review in Sherry, 2006). Although attempts to establish relationships among ecology, cognition, and brain structures have not always produced unambiguous results (see Roth, Brodin, Smulders, LaDage, & Pravosudov, 2010; Sherry, 2005), this approach, sometimes called *neuroecology*, is nevertheless an increasingly well-established part of comparative cognitive neuroscience (Sherry, 2006).

The research just reviewed compares species quantitatively: is Species A better at some class of cognitive task than Species B? An equally important kind of comparative research compares species qualitatively: does the performance of Species A and B change in the same way with changes in some independent variable? For example, does memory improve as time studying the sample increases? Similar patterns of change in performance with study time would be evidence for a common memory process, even if one species performs better than another at all values of the variables tested (Papini, 2008). This use of systematic variation is beautifully illustrated by the work of Wright and colleagues on *serial position effects* in people, monkeys, and pigeons (Wright, 2006).

The serial position effect is a classic finding in human memory: when people learn a list of several items, those at the beginning and end of the list are generally remembered best, the *primacy* and *recency* effects, respectively. Wright and colleagues (Wright, Santiago, Sands, Kendrick, & Cook, 1985) studied memory for lists of visual items using *serial probe recognition*. So that the samples would be meaningless to all species, kaleidoscope patterns were used for the people. Four samples were presented one at a time. A retention interval followed the fourth sample and then a single probe item was presented, either a randomly chosen item from this list or an item from some past list. The subject was rewarded for indicating correctly whether the probe was from the list. An ITI ensued followed by a new list and a test of another randomly chosen list position.

Serial position curves of pigeons, monkeys, and people all change in the same way with retention interval (Fig. 2.4). Recency predominates

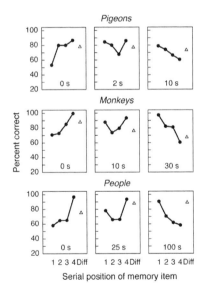

FIGURE **2.4.** Serial probe recognition performance of pigeons, rhesus monkeys, and people with lists of four items as a function of the position of the tested item in the list and the retention interval between the last item and the test, as indicated on each panel. Triangles are percent correct for indicating "different" on trials in which the test item had not appeared in the just-presented list. Redrawn from Wright et al. (1985) with permission.

at the shortest intervals and primacy at the longest; the classic U-shaped curve appears only at intermediate intervals. Performance for early items actually improves at longer intervals, indicating that at the shortest intervals immediate or short-term memory for the last item in the list inhibits or interferes with memory for later items. In this and other respects (see Wright, 2006), memory for lists of visual items works similarly in pigeon, monkey, and human. But the processes involved have very different time courses, as can be seen by comparing the durations of the medium and longest intervals shown for the three species in Figure 2.4. For instance, a U-shaped curve emerges after 2 seconds in pigeons, 10 seconds in monkeys, and 25 seconds in people. Similar dynamic serial position effects have been found in rats, but when the items are places in a radial maze they change over minutes rather than seconds (Harper, McLean, & Dalrymple-Alford, 1993).

Research on numerical cognition (Chapter 3) involves a theoretical assumption similar to that underlying this work: cognitive processes have distinctive "signatures" identifiable across species and tests with different materials and behavioral measures. The concept of functional similarity (Chapter 1) expresses the same assumption: a given process is identified in different species by looking for similar patterns of variation in some behavioral index when relevant factors are varied. For instance, people may be remembering words; jays, places where food was stored; and rats, odors, but identical patterns of data are evidence for shared memory processes.

Memory and Consciousness: Metacognition

People usually sense how well they know things. A driver knows whether to consult a map before setting out; a student knows what she needs to study for a test. Knowing what you remember is *metamemory*. It is one aspect of *metacognition*, which also includes knowing the accuracy of one's perceptual judgments, as in "I'm uncertain whether that bird is a red-tailed hawk." Literally, metacognition is cognition about cognition, that is, a form of higher order representation. Metacognitive judgments also seem to express a distinctive conscious state, a "feeling of knowing" or certainty. These attributes of metacognition in humans mean that claims to demonstrate it in animals are controversial (Carruthers, 2008). But even in humans the behavior associated with metacognition—seeking additional information or reporting on the strength of one's memory or perceptual certainty—need not result from explicit conscious assessment of a cognitive state. For instance, the student may have learned a rule for studying such as "start with the newest material." In other species, too, behavior consistent with metacognition may be understandable in terms of learned responses to publicly observable information rather than assessment of a private state (Carruthers, 2008; Hampton, 2009).

To illustrate, we look at a sample of tests of metamemory, beginning with the study of rhesus macaques diagrammed in Figure 2.5 (Hampton, 2001). Like many tests of metamemory, it incorporated both a direct measure of memory and a response that functioned as a report of memory strength. The direct test of memory was a delayed matching to sample task. The monkeys' sensitivity to their memory strength was tested at the end of retention intervals by offering a choice between taking the matching test and avoiding it. Correct matching responses were rewarded with a peanut; avoiding the memory test led to a primate pellet, a nonpreferred reward but better than the nonreward following matching errors. On 33% of trials the monkeys had no choice but to take the test. Matching performance

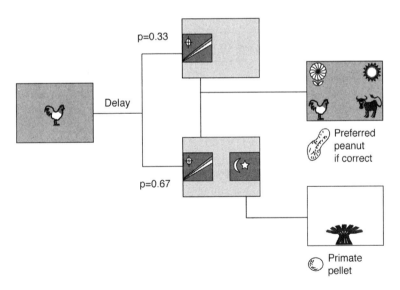

FIGURE **2.5.** Procedure for Hampton's (2001) test of metamemory for monkeys. A trial starts at the left with presentation of a sample (here, the rooster image). In the next stage, after a delay, the monkeys either chose between taking and avoiding the test of memory (lower of the two central panels, 67% of trials) or had no choice but to take the test of memory.

was worse on these "forced" trials than on chosen ones, consistent with use of metamemory in choosing whether to take the test.

But the behavior just described could result from using the length of the retention interval as a cue: after a short delay, matching is likely to be rewarded, whereas after long delays, when forgetting is more likely, avoiding the test leads to the better outcome. Importantly, however, tests with varied delays occurred only late in this experiment. Initial training was with a single intermediate delay; the monkeys were already performing better on chosen than forced tests. When the sample was then omitted on some trials, so there was nothing to remember, avoidance of the test immediately shot up. Finally, the pattern of data consistent with metamemory appeared as soon as long and short delays were introduced, again consistent with use of some internal or "private" cue correlated with memory strength. But this need not be awareness of memory strength as such, that is, metacognition in the strict sense. For instance, behavior might be controlled by the vividness of some briefly retained image of the sample (Carruthers, 2008; Hampton, 2009).

Although the exact nature of the representation or internal state controlling the monkeys' behavior is probably unknowable, this is one of the few studies to date ruling out control by obvious external, "public," cues (see also Smith, Shields, Allendoerfer, & Washburn, 1998). But studies that admit of control by such cues still show that—like the student following rules for effective studying—animals can behave adaptively when information is incomplete or uncertain without necessarily explicitly assessing their cognitive state. For example, in experiments that capture the spontaneous implicit use of metacognition in everyday life, children, apes (Call & Carpenter, 2001), and rhesus monkeys (Hampton, Zivin, & Murray, 2004) were confronted with two or more horizontal tubes, one of which held a reward. They more often looked into the tubes before choosing when they had not seen the tubes baited than when they had. But because the relevant options were presented simultaneously, behavior here could reflect the resolution of conflict between choosing a tube versus looking first rather than a metacognitive assessment as such (but see Call, 2010). The same is true of studies in which subjects (humans, monkeys, and a dolphin) choose whether to classify sounds or visual stimuli into one of two categories or to escape trials as too difficult. People say they escape when they feel uncertain (review in Smith, Shields, & Washburn, 2003). But although animals also escape most from the most difficult trials, behavior of all species in this paradigm can be predicted from the probabilities of reward for each response option at each stimulus without assuming any additional metacognitive process (Jozefowiez, Staddon, & Cerutti, 2009; Smith, Beran, Couchman, & Coutinho, 2008).

Metacognition has also been tested by training animals to "bet" whether they chose correctly *after* completing a task (Son & Kornell, 2005) and by offering them the chance to request hints when learning new tasks (Kornell, Son, & Terrace, 2007). Importantly, in some such studies monkeys trained on a metacognitive response in one task have used it appropriately in a novel one, that is, showing *transfer*. But although transfer implies the response was not controlled by cues specific to the original task, it could be based on a common self-generated cue such as correct choices being completed faster than incorrect ones (Hampton, 2009; Kornell et al., 2007). Again, the same is true of people in similar situations. Thus, notwithstanding attempts to demonstrate that animals share conscious metacognitive states such as uncertainty with humans (Smith et al., 2003; Smith & Washburn, 2005), the best conclusion from recent work is simply that some other species share with humans the ability to respond adaptively when memory or perception is unreliable. This behavior does not necessarily always reflect explicit assessment of a cognitive state, in either humans or other animals.

Episodic Memory

Episodic memory in humans is just what it says: memory for an episode of personal experience, what happened, where, and when, as distinct from *semantic memory*, or memory for facts and ideas. But over the years (see Tulving, 2005) the definition of episodic memory has come to include *autonoetic consciousness*, the sense of reexperiencing a consciously recollected episode, mentally traveling back in time to it. For example, most people have semantic knowledge of where and when they were born, but few claim episodic memory for the event. Because people with Alzheimer's disease and some kinds of hippocampal damage selectively lose the ability to acquire and express episodic memories, animal examples of episodic memory potentially have huge therapeutic applications. But if episodic memory necessarily includes autonoetic consciousness, it can never be conclusively demonstrated in nonhuman animals. The best that can be done is to look for so-called (Clayton & Dickinson, 1998) *episodic-like* memory, an integrated memory for what occurred, where, and when.

In the first demonstration of animal episodic-like memory (Clayton & Dickinson, 1998), Western scrub jays stored peanuts and wax worms, a greatly preferred food, in sand-filled trays. In two caching episodes 120 hours apart they cached peanuts in one side of a tray and wax worms in the other. Four hours after the second episode, that is, 124 hours after the first, birds were allowed to search for all the items. Worms cached 124 hours ago were distasteful as if rotten; 4 hours after caching they were fresh. Peanuts were always fresh. Thus, if the birds could remember where they had cached each food and how long ago, they should search for worms when worms had been cached more recently and peanuts otherwise. After a few trials this is what they did, and they continued choosing appropriately even when the experimenters secretly removed the items from the trays so that the birds could not be using cues such as odors. Control birds for which worms did not rot always searched for worms first. A series of studies with variations of this design (see de Kort, Dickinson, & Clayton, 2005) showed that the scrub jays' memory for their caches integrates location, time, and identity information and can be used flexibly, properties that further qualify it as episodic-like.

The work with scrub jays stimulated an outpouring of studies with other species, especially rats and mice, potential subjects for neurobiological analyses (see Crystal, 2009). In studies directly modeled on Clayton and Dickinson's, rats showed that they remember where and when they encountered chocolate ("what") in a radial maze (Babb & Crystal, 2005). Chocolate encountered on an initial visit to the maze was not replenished if the second visit was 1 hour later, but for second visits 25 hours later it was. After a number of trials of this treatment, the rats revisited the original chocolate location, which changed from trial to trial, after long but not short retention intervals. When the rats were subsequently made mildly ill after eating chocolate in their home cages during a 25-hour retention interval, they became less likely to revisit the old chocolate location. This finding indicates that memory includes the specific food, the value of which is flexibly updated with recent experience.

In the episodic-like memory studies described so far, "when" corresponded to "how long ago" because all trials were at the same time of day. In radial maze tests designed so both retention interval and time of day at initial exposure to the maze predict later availability of chocolate, rats preferentially encode "how long ago" (W. A. Roberts et al., 2008). However, when only time of day at encoding is relevant, they use that (Zhou & Crystal, 2009). But how well does either of these senses of "when" capture the temporal element of conscious recollections? Some (e.g., W. A. Roberts et al., 2008) argue that people refer episodic memories to specific times in the past, disqualifying memories that encode only "how long ago." Others (Zentall, Clement, Bhatt, & Allen, 2001) argue that because the jays and rats in these studies were trained over many trials to expect different outcomes after different retention intervals, these paradigms do not capture the spontaneous encoding that people do regardless of whether they expect a test of memory. Others (Eichenbaum, Fortin, Ergorul, Wright, & Agster, 2005) suggest that the "when" in human episodic memory is not time as such but spatial and/or temporal context: "during my Arctic cruise" rather than "in July 2008." This makes the study with rats depicted in Figure 2.2 a candidate demonstration of episodic-like memory because it shows that the animals spontaneously encode what is where in a specific context. More extensive studies from this perspective have employed rats' excellent olfactory memory to show that memory for a specific odor's location in a sequence ("list") of odors has important properties of episodic memory, including dependence on the hippocampus and dissociability from mere familiarity.

These studies (see Eichenbaum et al., 2005) used the fact that rats readily learn to use the odor in a bowl of sand as a cue to dig for buried food. After encountering a "list" (i.e., sequence) of five familiar odors, rats were tested for memory of item order (episodic-like memory) by presenting two odors from the list and rewarding choice of the earlier one. A test of relative familiarity consisted of choice between an odor from the list and a familiar odor not on it. To trace accuracy on both tasks over a range of levels, the animals' tendency to choose one bowl over the other was varied by varying reward size and/or effort required to dig in the correct bowl. The resulting functions mirrored those from human memory for words. In humans, episodic memory is identified with "remembering" a word was on a list, as distinct from merely knowing it had been presented, and tendency to identify a word as new versus old is manipulated with instructions to be more or less confident of the answer when saying "new." After hippocampal damage, both people and rats still perform well on the test of familiarity but not on tests of episodic memory. These and related studies of odor memory in rats provide perhaps the richest evidence for functional similarity between a kind of animal memory and human episodic-like memory.

In summary, there is now impressive evidence that animals encode multiple features of unique events just as humans encode multiple features of experienced episodes (for reviews see Crystal, 2009; Eacott & Easton, 2010). By focusing on the functional aspects of episodic memory, researchers using animals may be forcing human researchers to sharpen up their definition of it. But if autonoetic consciousness is an essential feature of human episodic memory, part of a faculty of "mental time travel" into both past and future allowing us to imagine and plan in a way other animals cannot, none of this evidence for common memory processes addresses the essence of episodic memory (Suddendorf & Corballis, 2008a). The discussion of planning in Chapter 3 revisits this issue.

Associative Learning

Associative learning in the broad or operational sense (Balsam & Gallistel, 2009) is the learning that results from exposure to relationships among events. Usually these are temporally predictive relationships, as when lightning flashes are followed by thunderclaps. To discover whether associative learning has occurred, the behavior of animals exposed to a predictive relationship is compared to that of other animals exposed to the same events unrelated, using a common test at the end of training. Because associative learning in its simplest forms is virtually universal among species, from fruit flies to people (Papini, 2008), Morgan's Canon (Chapter 1) dictates attempting to explain any novel example of learning as associative. Defining associative learning as a specialization for learning relationships among events means that such explanations are not necessarily always possible. Dead reckoning (Chapters 1 and 3) is not associative, nor at first glance is habituation or imitation (Chapter 4). In these cases no separable events are evident among which a relationship can be learned. In upcoming chapters we will encounter claims that some instances of learning are more than "merely" associative. Evaluating them requires knowing the basic facts about associative learning in the broad operational sense. What relationships do animals learn, what conditions foster this learning or interfere with it, and how is it expressed in behavior? Answers to these questions are sketched here. Fuller accounts are found in Bouton (2007) and Chapters 4, 6, and 11 of Shettleworth (2010a).

Associative learning is also used in a theoretical sense, to refer to a specific mechanism for learning: the formation of associations, hypothetical neural connections between event representations through which events excite or inhibit representations of their associates. Association formation is readily interpreted in neurobiological terms as strengthening of synaptic connections. For 40 years the most influential theoretical account of associative learning phenomena has been one based on this simple hypothetical process (Rescorla & Wagner, 1972). One recent "cognitive" theory of associative learning sketched later in this section suggests that it reflects explicit causal reasoning (e.g., "A causes B") or some analog to it (De Houwer, 2009; Shanks, 2010). Alternatively, the conclusion that A predicts the arrival of B may be the output from implicit mental computations on the remembered temporal sequence of As and Bs (Balsam & Gallistel, 2009).

Conditions for Learning

The prototypical example of associative learning is salivary conditioning in Pavlov's dogs, hence *Pavlovian* (or *classical*) *conditioning*. Pairing a relatively neutral stimulus such as a light or a sound (the *conditioned stimulus* or *CS*) with a biologically significant stimulus (the *unconditioned stimulus* or *US*) such as food, a shock, or access to a sexual partner results in a *conditioned response* (*CR*) to the CS which is appropriate to the US. If such a response is in fact due to the CS-US relationship, that is, learned associatively, it should not be shown by control animals after equivalent exposure to some other arrangement of CS and US, usually random presentations. The same learning principles apply to *instrumental* (or *operant*) conditioning, in which one of the animal's behaviors such as pressing a lever predicts a biologically significant stimulus, the reinforcer or reward.

Associative learning also occurs with events having no pre-experimental significance, as when a tone precedes a light or lemon flavor reliably occurs with anise. The learning in such cases may not be evident until one element of the association acquires biological significance. For instance, in within-event learning, if hungry rats drink a liquid flavored with both lemon and anise and lemon is then paired with food, they increase consumption of anise. Such examples underline the important distinction between learning (or memory) and *performance*, between what the animal knows and what it does. Here the animal learns that lemon and anise go together but does not reveal that learning in performance until lemon becomes significant. Within-event learning also underlines the essentially cognitive nature of even simple conditioning: the rat evidently acquires and stores a flexibly updatable representation of the anise-flavored lemonade.

So far the conditions for associative learning have been described informally, as "pairing" or "prediction." Some temporal contiguity (closeness in time) is usually necessary. Animals that experience only the CS or the US (or response and reinforcer) or experience them widely separated in time do not learn. The key is *contingency*, that is, one event predicts a change in probability of the other. The power of contingency is evident in demonstrations of the power of extra noncontingent USs to lead to *extinction*, loss of learned responding. For instance, when pigeons are key pecking for food, adding food presentations between lightings of the key reduces pecking. But contingency need not be perfect; instrumentally trained responses are maintained quite well when fewer than 100% of responses are rewarded, in *partial reinforcement*. Given enough training, animals learn subtle differences in US frequency or pattern.

Theory: Prediction Error

Since learning (or memory) presumably evolved so that animals could acquire locally appropriate information about the world, it ought to occur when there is a discrepancy between how things are and what the animal already knows. The importance of *prediction error* for associative learning is captured by the simple but amazingly productive model due to Rescorla and Wagner (1972) and diagrammed in Figure 2.6. It depicts the growth of hypothetical associative strength (V) underlying conditioned responding over CS-US pairings (trials) toward an asymptote (λ). The learning curve is negatively accelerated because the change in associative strength on a trial (ΔV) decreases the closer the total existing associative strength (ΣV) is to the asymptote, that is, the less the prediction error. The parameters α and β reflect the fact that learning rate

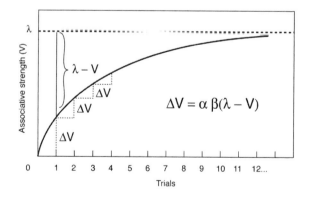

$$\Delta V = \alpha \beta(\lambda - V)$$

FIGURE **2.6.** The equation for the Rescorla-Wagner model and how it generates a negatively accelerated learning curve (heavy line). Short dotted lines show ΔV for the first four trials, illustrating how it decreases with decreases in the prediction error ($\lambda - V$), diagrammed as the distance between the existing associative strength, V, and the maximum possible, the asymptote, λ.

generally also depends on the strength or conspicuousness of the CS and US, respectively.

By making the effect of a trial with a given CS depend on the total existing associative strength, the Rescorla-Wagner model accounts for the phenomenon of *blocking*. In a typical example, animals first learn that a light predicts food. Then a tone is presented with the light so that the light+tone compound now predicts food. A control group has the same number of light+tone food presentations. When both groups are then tested with the tone alone, the controls show more conditioned responding. Tone learning in the first group, the blocking group, is blocked by prior training with the light. Informally, for animals in this group the tone adds no new information about the US. In terms of the Rescorla-Wagner model, the tone and the light are separate CSs that acquire associative strength individually as described by the equation in Figure 2.6 with ΣV equal to the total tone+light strength at the beginning of a compound trial. In the blocking group the light has substantial strength when tone+light training begins, so there is less strength left for the tone than in the control group.

This model also accounts for *overshadowing*: if two CSs are compounded (i.e., presented together) from the outset of training, less is learned about either than if it is trained alone for the same number of trials. The reader is invited to work out why. Notice that the model treats complex stimuli as a sum of elements rather than as a unique configuration. In the alternative *configural* approach, responding to B following training with A+B reflects the similarity of B alone to A+B, that is, conditioned responding *generalizes*, as discussed more in the final section of this chapter. On an elemental approach, animals should not be able to learn a task in which A and B are each separately reinforced while the A+B compound is not; for example, chocolate or cinnamon flavored food are both nutritious but a food with both flavors is poisonous. But animals do learn such discriminations, a fact readily accounted for if compounds are configurations. An elemental view, however, can account for the same results if compounds include a separate configural element. Overall each view has its particular strengths and weaknesses, suggesting that animals may sometimes treat compound stimuli as configurations and sometimes as the sum of elements.

The simple mechanical process embodied in the Rescorla-Wagner model can, in effect, extract the best predictors from complex sequences of events. For example, suppose a light is followed by a US on the 50% of trials when it is accompanied by a tone, but it is not followed by the US when accompanied by a clicker on the other 50% of trials. The tone is the best predictor here, so it will support much more responding than the light. But when light+tone and light+clicker each predict the US on 50% of trials, the light is the best predictor and accordingly elicits the most CRs. Responding to the light reflects its predictive value relative to that of other cues in the situation, not its own frequency of pairing with the US (which is the same in both arrangements just described).

The importance of predictiveness extends to higher order arrangements of cues. As an example from instrumental conditioning, if while a tone is on bar pressing is reinforced but chain pulling is unreinforced and while the tone is off the reverse is true, rats learn to bar press during the tone and pull the chain otherwise. The tone is an *occasion setter* or *modulator*. Comparable conditional control develops in Pavlovian conditioning. Occasion setters may be contextual cues such as distinctively decorated chambers or different spatial locations. Learning about occasion setters helps to insure that behavior is appropriate to the circumstances. Such conditional control of behavior has a role in naturally occurring situations, as when a low-ranking male baboon readily approaches females in the absence of a dominant male but not in his presence.

Temporal Factors

In addition to predictiveness, associative learning depends on temporal factors. Other things being equal, conditioning is improved with a shorter gap between CS and US (the *CS-US interval*) or response and reinforcer (the reinforcer delay). CS and US can be simultaneous, as in the example with lemon and anise. In Pavlovian conditioning, the CS-US interval over which any learning occurs depends on the particular CS, US, and species. For most mammals, tasting a novel flavor and experiencing gastric distress even hours afterward leads to rejection of the flavor (flavor aversion learning). Most other examples of conditioning require much shorter CS-US intervals, perhaps just a few seconds. When the CS is extended in time, for example a 30-second tone with the US at the end (*delay conditioning*), the CR is eventually shown primarily near the time of the US, an example of timing a stimulus (Chapter 3). Animals also time a temporal gap between CS and US, as when a tone comes on briefly and the US is 30 seconds later (*trace conditioning*; delayed reinforcement in instrumental conditioning). The time between episodes of CS and US, the *intertrial interval* (or *ITI*), also matters: with a given CS-US interval, conditioning proceeds more rapidly the longer the ITI. Conditioned taste aversion or fear conditioning (i.e., a CS predicts shock) can occur in a single trial, but with systems that take more than a few trials the ratio between ITI and CS-US interval is critical. CRs appear after fewer trials when the ITI is relatively long, another effect of predictiveness: under such conditions the CS gives more useful information about the time of occurrence of the US.

Belongingness and Behavior Systems

Conditioned flavor aversion in rats was the first well-studied example of *belongingness*, the observation that some pairs of events are especially readily associated. When the US is gastric distress produced by mild poison, a flavor experienced hours beforehand is associated with it and later avoided, whereas a sound or visual cue experienced in the same relationship with illness is not. However, lights or sounds presented while a rat drinks a flavored liquid later suppress drinking with an immediate shock US but not delayed illness. Belongingness, or biological relevance, is a general feature of associative learning, one illustration of the adaptiveness of cognitive mechanisms. Here, rapid learning of a relationship between food-identifying cues and later consequences of eating could be important in guiding food choice, especially in an omnivorous animal like a rat.

Similarly, the *performance rules* or effects on behavior of classical as well as instrumental conditioning make adaptive sense. The effects of instrumental conditioning are straightforward: behaviors with fitness-increasing outcomes such as food or access to a mate generally increase in frequency and those with fitness-threatening outcomes such as pain or contact with a predator decrease. In Pavlovian conditioning, CRs are usually related to both the US-specific behavior system and the features of the CS. A striking illustration is *autoshaping* with pigeons, in which lighting the pecking key is followed by food or water regardless of whether the bird pecks. With food US, birds that are both hungry and thirsty begin to peck the key as if they were eating it, whereas with water as US they press their beaks against the key as if drinking it. And if the CS is a tone or other diffuse stimulus, they increase activity in its presence.

Contents of Learning

Traditional associations are unidimensional, but they may link rich representations of CS and US. For instance, revaluing reinforcers after training shows that US representations may include both the value and the quality of the US. Thus, when rats that have associated a light with food pellets and a tone with sucrose are made mildly ill in their home cages after eating pellets, CRs to the light decrease in a subsequent test while those to the tone are unaffected. Importantly, this effect appears in unreinforced tests, revealing the contents of original learning as opposed to new learning that the light predicts disgusting food. Specific foods can also be revalued by satiation or deprivation.

Analogous revaluation effects occur in instrumental conditioning, where they imply that instrumental learning involves more than single associative links. Historically instrumental learning was seen as reflecting stimulus-response (S-R) associations: reinforcement "stamps in" an associative link between situational stimuli and a response. (In contrast, Pavlovian conditioning is S-S, links between CS and US representation.) But this account leaves no role for a representation of the reinforcer after learning, whereas revaluation effects comparable to those just described for the Pavlovian case show that an updatable memory of the value and quality of the reinforcer does control behavior after training. This supports an account (Dickinson, 2008) on which the content of instrumental learning includes both belief that the response leads to the reinforcer (a response-outcome association) and a desire for the reinforcer. Responding results from an implicit reasoning process, for example, "Bar pressing leads to food, I want that food, therefore I press." Although such flexible implicit reasoning accounts for many aspects of instrumental behavior (see Dickinson, 2008), instrumentally learned responses can become inflexible or habit-like after extensive training, lending partial support to the S-R account.

Theory: Associations or Propositions?

The Rescorla-Wagner model shows how excitatory and inhibitory associations can produce behavior that tracks the causal structure of the world without representing it as such. In contrast, on some contemporary accounts (see De Houwer, 2009; Shanks, 2010) even Pavlovian conditioning reflects a reasoning-like process, if not explicit propositions. Much of the supporting evidence comes from studies of human causal learning in which people learn about relationships between such things as foods and allergic reactions. Key evidence for reasoning here comes from *backward blocking*, which involves the opposite sequence events to those in a traditional blocking experiment. Subjects might first learn that rhubarb+strawberries produces illness and then learn that rhubarb alone produces the same symptom. On the Rescorla-Wagner model, this experience should not change the tendency to attribute illness to strawberries. In fact, however, people behave as if reasoning that because rhubarb alone causes illness, strawberries don't. But analogous findings with rats can be explained on an associative account (see Shanks, 2010). Further challenges are raised by evidence that backward or forward blocking can be modified by teaching subjects beforehand about the maximum possible value of a US and by reports (Waldmann, Cheng, Hagmayer, & Blaisdell, 2008) that rats behave as if reasoning in novel instrumental paradigms. Such findings fuel an ongoing debate about the extent to which unconscious automatic processes or more "cognitive" proposition-like processes produce the phenomena of associative learning. As with many such debates, the answer may be that both kinds of mechanisms are at play in different species and/or circumstances.

Concluding Remarks

Even on a traditional connectionist approach and more so on some contemporary theories, associative learning provides animals with subtle and flexible knowledge about relationships among events. Among other things, multiple features of events and conditional relationships among them may be learned, and learned behavior can change with changing outcome values. The behavior resulting from associative learning is not mere automatic "spit and twitches" (Rescorla, 1988). Regardless of whether they explicitly represent causal relationships, animals can track them very well. The richness and variety of phenomena resulting from associative learning set a high bar for claims that apparently "more cognitive" examples of learning rely on other processes.

Discrimination, Classification, and Concepts

Whether through learning or otherwise, animals must behave differently toward different things: adaptive behavior depends on discrimination. Examples of discrimination training were mentioned in the last section. In the simplest, reinforcement follows one stimulus or action and not another, but we have also seen conditional discrimination and training with multiple cues having different predictive values. The basic principles are the same whether discrimination training is instrumental or Pavlovian. Most examples in this section involve instrumental training.

The simplest discrimination training requires a rewarded stimulus (S+) and an unrewarded one (S–). S+ and S– may be presented simultaneously and the animal chooses between them, or they may be presented one at a time (*successive discrimination training*), and rates or latencies of responding are compared. In *discrimination reversal learning*, animals are trained with given S+ and S– to some criterion such as 80% of responses correct. Then S+ and S– reverse roles until criterion is achieved again, and so on. In *learning set* experiments, when one discrimination is learned to criterion, S+ and S– are replaced with novel cues and training recommences. Both procedures test whether animals "learn to learn," improving on successive discriminations toward the optimum of no more than one error per problem. Such improvement indicates that more is involved in discrimination learning than acquiring associative strength to S+ and S–.

At one time successive reversal and learning set seemed to offer ways to compare species on intelligence, with quicker improvement indicating higher intelligence. However, among other problems, species rankings can depend on exactly how the tests are done (contextual variables), and performance of any given species can also depend on the stimuli used. In learning set, for example, rats show markedly more improvement with olfactory or spatial than with visual discriminations. Comparing species on reversal learning is also appealing because it seems to tap cognitive flexibility, which should be adaptive in highly seasonal environments or frequently shifting social groups. Of course, any attempt to compare species on such a hypothetical general cognitive trait requires multiple tasks, as in Amici, Aureli, and Call's (2008) comparison of seven primate species with different social systems.

The flip side of discrimination is *generalization*, responding similarly to different stimuli. Some degree of generalization is necessary: no two blueberries, babies, or encounters with laboratory stimuli are exactly the same, but it may be adaptive to treat them as such. The balance between discriminating and generalizing is revealed by varying the training stimulus along one of its physical dimensions to trace out a *generalization gradient*. In the example in Figure 2.7 pigeons were trained to peck a key illuminated with a 550 nm light. When the wavelength was varied around this value, the rate of pecking decreased smoothly on either side of S+ ("Control" curve). The figure also includes an example of *peak shift*: birds trained with the same 550 nm S+ and 570 nm as S– pecked maximally not at S+ but at a wavelength displaced away from S–. *Positive behavioral contrast* is also shown: responding to S+ was greater when it was alternated with the unreinforced S– than in the control group trained only with S+. Generalization and peak shift are ubiquitous, characteristic of both natural or untrained and associatively learned behavior (Ghirlanda & Enquist, 2003).

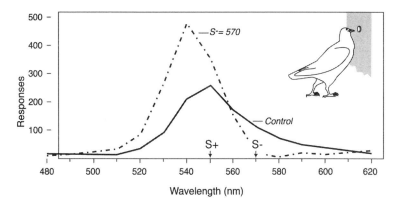

FIGURE **2.7.** Wavelength generalization and peak shift in pigeons. The control group was simply reinforced for pecking at a key illuminated by 550 nm. The other group learned a successive discrimination in which it was also nonreinforced when the key was illuminated with 570 nm, the S–. Redrawn from Hanson (1959).

Category Discrimination

Armed with information about discrimination and generalization, we can analyze what happens when animals are trained in *category discriminations*, that is, with large sets of S+'s and S–'s. The simplest such tasks involve *perceptual categories*. Here the categories to be discriminated differ in some surface feature(s), such as being people or fish. In an early example (Herrnstein, Loveland, & Cable, 1976), pigeons learned to discriminate 40 pictures with trees from 40 without trees. The acid test of genuine category learning is transfer: does the animal respond appropriately to new instances (*exemplars)* of the categories? In cases like those just described, the answer to this question is generally "yes"; there is transfer but it is not necessarily perfect. It arises from some combination of memorizing something about the training slides and generalizing from them. What is memorized could be each slide as a whole or features common to multiple slides or perhaps a prototype or average of each category. In cases like presence versus absence of trees, no single feature can do the job. For instance, trees have trunks, but they are different colors; trees don't all have green leaves, but celery does. Thus, to base effective category discrimination on feature learning, multiple features must be combined in some way.

One alternative to feature learning is memorizing each exemplar as a whole. For pigeons, this possibility is supported by results of *pseudocategory* training, in which members of a large and diverse set of pictures are assigned arbitrarily to be S+'s and S−'s. Pigeons learn to respond correctly to 320 or more such items and remember them for up to 2 years (Cook et al., 2005). Evidence that both memorizing and generalizing play a role in perceptual category learning comes from experiments (Bhatt, Wasserman, Reynolds, & Knauss, 1988) in which pigeons learned to discriminate among four categories: cats, flowers, cars, and chairs. Not surprisingly, the pigeons learned more slowly the more items per category. However, having learned to a given criterion, birds trained with more items showed better transfer. Again this is not surprising: the more items or features of a class that have been memorized, the greater the possibilities for generalization to new members of the class. Such memorizing can be quick: birds could learn the same four categories with each exemplar shown only once. When old exemplars were presented for a second time, they were classified more accurately than new ones, suggesting that the birds did memorize each exemplar as a whole.

Although photographs of objects and scenes may be useful for revealing processes involved in categorizing real-world objects, for understanding the details of these processes artificially composed categories are indispensable. For instance, consider learning a category in which some members have features typical of an alternative category, as in learning the egg-laying, duck-billed platypus is a mammal, not a bird. When human subjects learn to classify simple shapes into two sets with this property, they improve quickly on the typical category members but initially perform below chance on the exceptions, classifying them in the opposite category. Eventually the learning curve for exceptions catches up to that for typical members. This pattern, described as abstraction of general properties followed by learning of exceptions, is also shown by rhesus monkeys (Smith, Chapman, & Redford, 2010) and pigeons (Cook & Smith, 2006), suggesting it is very general among vertebrates. The superiority of typical items points to a role for generalization across features or overall resemblance among category members.

In contrast is the problem of learning to classify two-component patterns such as stripes with varying widths and tilts. Two categories can be defined by a simple rule; for instance, all stripes wider than so much are in one class, all those narrower in the other. Here only one feature need be learned about: width. The same patterns can be divided in what is called a linearly separable way, such that if they are arranged in a square, narrow to wide and less to more tilted, a diagonal line across the array separates the two categories. Here neither width nor tilt alone is enough; how a particular width is categorized depends on its tilt. Information integration is required. People and rhesus monkeys learn rule-based categories faster than linearly separated categories of the same stimuli (Smith, Beran, Crossley, Boomer, & Ashby, 2010), showing that "rule-based" superiority need not imply reliance on a verbal rule. However, pigeons learn both kinds of categories at the same rate (Smith et al., 2011), indicating they do not necessarily rely on a single diagnostic feature even when one is available (see also Lea & Wills, 2008).

Functional Categories and Equivalence Classes

Although early demonstrations of animal perceptual category learning (e.g., Herrnstein et al., 1976) were described as studies of concept learning, as we have seen they need not involve the kind of deeper connections among exemplars that would normally be described as conceptual. *Functional categories* come closer. Items in a functional category share an associate but not necessarily any perceptible features. For instance, oranges and peas belong to the perceptual category "round things" but also to the functional category "foods" along with lamb chops and samosas. Social relationships such as family membership define important natural functional categories for some species. Their distinguishing quality is that exemplars are linked in such a way that they change in value together. Thus, in baboon society, a whole family shares a dominance status relative to other families; occasional battles between a few members change the status of all (Cheney & Seyfarth, 2007).

Pigeons can learn functional categories in the laboratory through successive reversal training with pseudocategories. For instance, unrelated pictures 1–12 are Category 1 and pictures 13–24, Category 2. Initially Category 1 is S+ and Category 2 S–. Once this is learned, the 1's become S– and the 2's S+, and so on. The significance of each picture has to be relearned individually in early reversals, but eventually exposure to the new value of one or a few category members immediately transfers to all. The minimal case is *many to one matching to sample*, in which each of two or three different samples is associated with the same correct choice. The mechanism responsible for transfer among category members here is *mediated generalization*, that is, generalization through the mediation of their common associate.

Relational Categories

So far we have looked at categorization based on physical features. An arguably more complex cognitive achievement is categorizing things on the basis of their relationship, for example, mother and daughter or, in the best-studied case, same versus different. Classifying something as, say, a person or a tree, involves first-order representation, whereas classifying two or more items as the same involves a higher order representation, one that transcends perceptible features of individual items. People have a domain-general concept of sameness versus difference that extends not only across modalities but to abstract content, as when comparing theories of learning. This relationship is categorical: things are either the same or they are different, although their differences may be subtle or conspicuous, few or many.

At first glance, delayed matching to sample requires a concept of sameness, but this is not necessarily correct. For one thing, the stimulus matching the sample is relatively more familiar, having been presented more recently than other options. For another, not all animals that successfully match with one small set of stimuli immediately match when transferred to a new set. Monkeys do much better than pigeons in this regard, but some corvids also transfer quite well. Pigeons eventually acquire a generalized ability to match after training with many different matching problems (Wright, Cook, & Rivera, 1988). At first they apparently learn specific S-R associations: "if the sample was red, peck red; if it was green, peck green…" Consistent with this interpretation, they learn literal matching no faster than *symbolic* (or *conditional*) *matching to sample* in which, for example, pecking a circle is reinforced after a red sample and pecking a square after a green sample.

For genuine relational categorization, most interest has focused on the simultaneous same/different task. Here the subject classifies sets of items as all the same or not. Pigeons do not learn this task when started with displays of only two items (e.g., AA, BB, or CC,…as "same" vs. AB, CB, etc. as "different"). However, when started with larger displays, usually 4x4 arrays of icons on a computer screen (Fig. 2.8), they do learn to choose "same" for 16 identical icons and "different" for a display of 16 different ones. This performance transfers to displays of 16 novel icons. It also transfers to smaller sets if they are introduced gradually, eventually to sets of two novel images (Wasserman & Young, 2010). Monkeys also perform well in this task, after less extensive training.

Although the findings suggest that animals can acquire a relational concept, performance on "different" displays having fewer than the maximum different items reveals that accuracy is graded: with displays like that on the right in Figure 2.8 the task is harder the more items are the same (for instance, if eight of the 16 icons were cows). In contrast, people equally well classify displays with even one different item (e.g., 15 cows and one car) as "different." Thus while people employ a categorical (all-or-none) concept, monkeys and pigeons apparently discriminate perceptual variability. Importantly, though, people still show evidence of the latter process: they classify displays as "different" more quickly the more different items they contain. The shared perceptual classification mechanism may be the basis of the abstract and general same/different concept possibly unique to humans and possibly mediated by language. Such a species difference is consistent with the claim that the ability to form higher-order

"Same"   "Different"

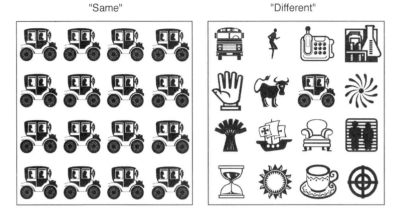

FIGURE **2.8.** Examples of stimuli used to train pigeons in same/different discriminations. After Wasserman et al. (1995) with permission.

representations is uniquely human (Chapter 5 and Penn et al., 2008). However, the latency effect just described indicates that this ability exists alongside evolutionarily older first-order perceptual classification.

Relational matching with sets of two items can be seen as analogical reasoning: AA is analogous to CC, whereas AB is analogous to CD. Thus some importance has been attached to the finding that chimpanzees can acquire two-item relational matching without initial training on larger displays, whereas other primates (baboons and rhesus macaques) seem to need it. However, contextual variables turn out to be important here, raising a caution against too readily accepting species differences that fit our preconceptions. Rhesus monkeys learn when trained with displays of two items from the outset if different sized rewards are given for correct "same" versus correct "different" responses (*differential outcomes training*; Flemming, Thompson, Beran, & Washburn, 2011). But these and similar effects of other procedural modifications (see Flemming et al., 2011) also indicate that monkeys need extra supports to succeed at two-item relational matching.

Concluding Remarks

This section has concluded that there may not be a yes or no answer to the question of whether other species have abstract same/different categorization. Whereas a basic perceptual classification ability seems to be shared across species, categorical same/different discrimination may not be. This finding illustrates the importance of a bottom-up or elemental approach to global abilities, a principle that has already popped up in the discussion of episodic-like memory and metacognition. We will meet it again in the next chapters.

At the same time, the importance of contextual variables to monkeys' success when trained solely on two-item same/different discrimination (or analogical reasoning) indicates that conclusions about species differences should always be somewhat provisional. Some species may need extra supports to succeed at a task that others learn quickly, but it also has to be considered that such procedural modifications change the fundamental nature of the task. Only further research will reveal which is the case in this instance.

Finally, this section has also introduced the principle that transfer tests with perceptually novel material are necessary for discovering what has been learned in a categorization or concept-formation task. In the next two chapters we will see this principle applied in specific cognitive domains, for example, in testing whether animals have abstract numerical or social concepts.

Suggestions for Further Reading

Bouton, M. E. (2007). *Learning and Behavior*. Sunderland, MA: Sinauer Associates.

Eacott, M. J., & Easton, A. (2010). Episodic memory in animals: Remembering which occasion. *Neuropsychologia*, *48*, 2273–2280.

Hampton, R. R. (2009). Multiple demonstrations of metacognition in nonhumans: Converging evidence or multiple mechanisms? *Comparative Cognition and Behavior Reviews*, *4*, 17–28.

Rescorla, R. A. (1988). Pavlovian conditioning: It's not what you think it is. *American Psychologist*, *43*, 151–160.

Shanks, D. R. (2010). Learning: From association to cognition. *Annual Review of Psychology*, *61*, 273–301.

Shettleworth, S. J. (2010). *Cognition, Evolution, and Behavior* (2nd ed.). New York: Oxford University Press. Chapters 3–7.

Wasserman, E. A., & Young, M. E. (2010). Same-different discrimination: The keel and backbone of thought and reasoning. *Journal of Experimental Psychology: Animal Behavior Processes*, *36*, 3–22.

Wright, A. A. (2006). Memory processing. In E. A. Wasserman & T. R. Zentall (Eds.), *Comparative Cognition: Experimental Explorations of Animal Intelligence* (pp. 164–185). New York: Oxford University Press.

Zentall, T. R., Wasserman, E. A., Lazareva, O. F., Thompson, R. R. K., & Rattermann, M. J. (2008). Concept learning in animals. *Comparative Cognition and Behavior Reviews*, *3*, 13–45.

CHAPTER 3

Physical Cognition

How do animals find their way around? Do animals tell time? Can they count? Or plan ahead? What do they understand about tools? Such questions about physical knowledge are the subject of this chapter. Where, when, and how much are fundamental aspects of the worlds of all species. The cognitive mechanisms involved in processing them have been studied in a wide range of species at levels from neurobiology to natural behavior. Research on spatial cognition, timing, and sensitivity to numerosity provides evidence for modularity in cognition, that is, for mechanisms devoted to processing, storing, and acting on specific kinds of information. But we have not left behind the processes discussed in Chapter 2. A central question in comparative cognition is to what extent associative learning can explain the phenomena of physical and social (Chapter 4) cognition. Or are specialized processes such as understanding physical causation, insight, or foresight required?

Spatial Cognition: How Do Animals Find Their Way Around?

Wayfinding is a nearly universal problem in animal life. When important resources are separated in space, animals must find their way between them without getting lost. The study of how they do it embraces the small movements of invertebrates and the continent-spanning migrations of birds, even the choices of humans in virtual environments, specialized sensory mechanisms such as magnetoreception, and some of the most detailed neurobiological analyses of any behavior (see Jeffery, 2010;

McNaughton, Battaglia, Jensen, Moser, & Moser, 2006). We focus here on behavioral studies of fairly short-distance orientation, but the same framework applies to homing and migration (Bingman & Cheng, 2005) and organizes the data which neurobiological studies aim to explain.

For over half a century a central question in the study of spatial cognition has been, "Do animals have cognitive maps?" This is an anthropomorphic question, in that many people feel they use cognitive maps, analogs of physical maps in the mind's eye. A physical map is an *allocentric* representation of space; locations on it are related to some external frame of reference independent of the observer. (An observer-centered framework is *egocentric*.) Maps that accurately represent distances and directions can be used to plan new trips. Accordingly, a hypothetical cognitive map allows its possessor to take shortcuts or novel routes to familiar goals. But mechanisms other than an overall allocentric representation of space can explain the results of most, perhaps all, tests of cognitive mapping. We look at such mechanisms first.

Elements of Spatial Orientation

Because it combines distance and direction, spatial information is vector-like (see Fig. 3.1b). For example, a chipmunk might remember that "Home is under the pine tree 3 meters northwest of the big rock." However, efficient travel does not demand information about space as such. Some animals home by following chemical trails laid down on the outward journey. Our chipmunk might memorize a route, that is, which way to turn and how far to run from each of a series of rocks, bushes, and so on. Route learning permits efficient travel among familiar places, but it is a form of stimulus-response association, S-R learning. Our chipmunk might use the pine tree as a *beacon* which it need only approach to find the burrow. A beacon (see Fig. 3.1a) may be associated with a goal or innately attractive like cues from a receptive female. In any case, approaching one is a response to its value rather than use of spatial information as such.

When a goal is displaced from objects that indicate its location, for example, if the chipmunk's burrow were somewhere between the rock and the pine tree, those objects function as *landmarks*. To use an object as a landmark, the animal must encode the vector between it and the goal (Fig. 3.1b). It can then return to the goal by continuously moving to reduce the discrepancy between the current and remembered distance and direction from the landmark. Goals can be relocated most accurately using two or more landmarks (Kamil & Cheng, 2001), but how they are used varies with species. Clark's nutcrackers remember the distances and bearings to landmarks from buried seeds, with bearings (angles and

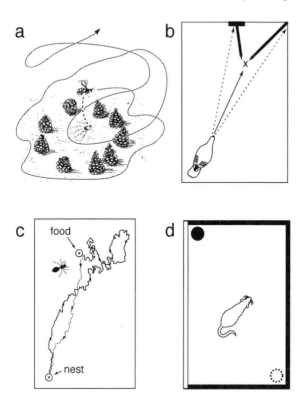

FIGURE **3.1.** Examples of four primary wayfinding mechanisms. (*a*) The nest of the digger wasp functions as a *beacon*. After Tinbergen (1951) with permission. (*b*) Hypothetical vectors involved in computing the location of a hidden goal (*x*) after training with a conspicuous *landmark* (black bar). The corner of the search space is a second landmark. Dotted arrows are perceived self-landmark vectors, and heavy arrows are remembered landmark-goal vectors from which the required movement toward the hidden goal can be computed (thin arrow). (*c*) *Path integration* by a desert ant; after travelling from the nest by a wavy path, the ant runs straight back with food (dashed path). Redrawn from Muller and Wehner (1988) with permission. (*d*) Rectangular arena with one white and three black walls. Black dot indicates the location of buried food (the goal). The disoriented rat will search equally often at the diagonally opposite corner (dotted circle), relying on the *geometry* of the enclosure and ignoring local cues of wall color.

directions) encoded especially precisely. Honeybees behave as if record-ing a "snapshot" from the goal and moving to match the current view with the snapshot. Thus, if landmarks near a goal are made bigger or smaller, honeybees search for it farther away or closer, respectively.

Dead reckoning (equivalently *path integration*) was introduced in Chapter 1 with the description of foraging by desert ants. Dead reckoning is egocentric: the animal moving out from a home base continuously records its distance and direction from the start so even if it has been turning this way and that, it can run straight back home at any moment without needing beacons or landmarks (Fig. 3.1c). The egocentric nature of dead reckoning is evident in the observations described in Chapter 1. Once it finds food, if we move the ant with its prey 50 meters or so to one side, it runs off the same distance and direction as an undisturbed ant and then starts circling around as if searching for the nest (Wehner & Srinivasan, 1981). Ants tell direction by the position of the sun, using their internal clock to correct for time of day. They measure distance by counting steps, correcting for the slopes of any hills along the way (Wittlinger et al., 2007). Mammals, including people, also use dead reckoning, but they sense changes in direction using the ves-tibular system of the inner ear (Etienne & Jeffery, 2004). Rotating a rat or a person in darkness a few times disrupts the sense of direction.

If a small rodent, bird, fish, monkey, ant, or human toddler who finds a goal in one corner of a rectangular enclosure like that shown in Figure 3.1d, is then disoriented (e.g., by rotation) and allowed to relocate the goal, the subject visits the correct corner and the diagonally opposite corner equally often (Cheng & Newcombe, 2005). When no features distinguish the correct corner, this observation reveals sensitivity to some correlate of the *geometry* (i.e., shape) of the enclosure. But even with disambiguating features such as a distinctively colored wall (Fig. 3.1d), subjects without extensive training still make as many diagonal errors as correct responses. This finding was originally (Cheng, 1986) seen as evidence for a geometric module that preempts control of spatial behavior in disoriented animals, but how animals encode and respond to "geometry" is debated. Possibili-ties include using a local cue consisting of the left-right position (sense) and relative length of walls at the goal, a global cue such as position relative to the long axis of the enclosure, and a view-matching mechanism. The last of these is egocentric rather than a record of shape as such, encoding how the environmental panorama looks from the goal and continuously moving so as to reduce the discrepancy between the present and remem-bered views (Fig. 3.2). View-matching models are increasingly prominent as possible accounts of spatial behavior (Cheung, Stürzl, Zeil, & Cheng,

View
from goal

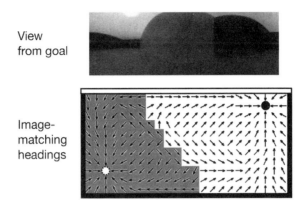

Image-
matching
headings

FIGURE **3.2.** (*Top*) Panoramic image of the arena in Figure 3.1d as seen from the goal. The 360° view is unwrapped with the goal corner to right of center. (*Bottom*) Predicted headings of a creature moving at each point to maximally reduce the discrepancy between the current view and that at the goal. Such a creature will generally arrive at the correct corner or its geometric equivalent. After Stürzl et al. (2008) with permission.

2008; Sheynikhovich, Chavarriaga, Strosslin, Arleo, & Gerstner, 2009). Importantly, they are strictly mechanistic, specifying input-output rules that can be implemented in robots. Geometry, beacons, and landmarks are not represented as such but are simply part of the visual panorama.

Integration

Real-world environments are typically rich with spatial cues. Which are used, and how is information from them combined? This question is typically answered by dissociating two or more cues so that some point one way and some another, as in Tinbergen's (1932/1972) classic study of digger wasps. These insects dig burrows, lay eggs, and bring caterpillars to provision their young. To see whether the wasps used distant or nearby landmarks, Tinbergen made a circle of pinecones around the entrance to a burrow (Fig. 3.1a). After the owner had made several foraging trips, the pinecones were moved to one side while she was away. When she returned, the wasp landed in the center of the pinecone circle and searched there, even though the burrow was nearby. Here local landmarks are more important than distant ones or the beacon of the burrow entrance. However, the wasp must have used distant landmarks to find the pinecones in the first place. In another example of such hierarchical cue use, when a hamster first finds food to hoard in a novel arena, it homes using dead reckoning but then learns the locations of landmarks. When landmarks are moved slightly, an experienced animal follows them, ignoring dead reckoning. But if the landmarks are removed or moved too far, the animal ignores them and falls back on dead reckoning (Etienne, 2003).

Rather than being used separately, information from distinct spatial cues may be averaged (Cheng, Shettleworth, Huttenlocher, & Rieser, 2007). Subjects may search between the locations indicated by two cues, but closer to that indicated by the more informative one, as if computing a weighted average of landmark-goal vectors like those illustrated in Figure 3.1b. Landmarks closer to a goal permit more accurate localization, and accordingly they are weighted more strongly than those farther away (Kamil & Cheng, 2001).

Associative Learning and Multiple Spatial Cues

In Tolman's (1948) classic proposal, cognitive mapping meant learning relationships among environmental stimuli, S-S learning, as opposed to route learning, the S-R learning thought more important at the time. Cognitive maps could be acquired without explicit reward, as when rats spontaneously learn the location of an object during exploration (Fig. 2.2 in Chapter 2). Similarly, in classic studies of *latent learning* rats evidently learned the layout of a maze by exploring it because they later learned to locate reward in it faster than naive rats. In the influential development by O'Keefe and Nadel (1978), cognitive maps were the outcome of a special learning system, the *locale system*, in the hippocampus of mammals and distinct from the *taxon system* responsible for associative learning. New information could be added to a cognitive map more or less indefinitely just as to a paper map. This property distinguishes cognitive maps from compound stimuli in conditioning, in which cues compete for a fixed pool of associative strength (Chapter 2).

Blocking—the preemption of learning by earlier-trained cues—is especially clear evidence for cue competition in learning. Accordingly, in numerous recent studies animals have been trained to find a goal with a single cue before receiving further training with a second cue added. This blocking group's accuracy in finding the goal with the second cue alone is then compared to that of a control group trained from the outset with both cues. Whether the blocking group performs worse than the controls in this test (i.e., whether blocking or a result more consistent with cognitive mapping is found) depends on the cues. When a rat learns to use a beacon to find the one dry location in a swimming pool, learning about added landmarks is blocked. Landmarks block other landmarks in this situation as well (Pearce, 2009). But consistent with the fact that dead reckoning seems to go on in parallel with orientation based on allocentric cues, experience homing by dead reckoning does not block learning about a beacon or landmark added later (Shettleworth & Sutton, 2005).

On first glance, geometry learning does not compete with learning about landmarks or beacons either (Pearce, 2009). For instance, disoriented rats trained to find food near a black stripe in a square enclosure transfer their learning about the stripe to a rectangular enclosure, but after further training in the rectangle they perform as well in tests with geometry alone (i.e., with the black stripe absent) as do rats trained in the striped rectangle from the outset (Wall, Botly, Black, & Shettleworth, 2004). This finding is consistent with the claim that learning the shape of an enclosure reflects a separate geometric module (Cheng, 1986). However, because subjects in such studies choose which corner to visit, they control the contingencies between cues and reward in a dynamic way. A formal model based on this fact shows that many findings are equally consistent with competition for learning between features such as the black stripe and cues defining geometry (Miller & Shettleworth, 2007; but see Pearce, 2009).

So Do Animals Have Cognitive Maps?

Traditional evidence for cognitive mapping is the ability to choose a novel shortcut or detour when a familiar path is blocked. Figure 3.3 depicts a classic test for rats. However, the setup has a serious flaw: the light near the goal is a beacon, so the fact that rats placed in the center of the "sunburst" maze tended to head toward the goal need not mean they had cognitive maps. Recent tests of cognitive mapping with rats (W. A. Roberts, Cruz, & Tremblay, 2007; Singer, Abroms, & Zentall, 2006) circumvented this problem by using completely enclosed mazes with local cues such as floor textures distinguishing the arms. By repeatedly traversing the maze, rats could learn where its parts were relative to one another based on these cues together with vestibular and proprioceptive cues. This information must somehow enable above-chance choice of appropriate novel paths, but it is debatable whether it should be called a cognitive map.

Because honeybees acquire extensive knowledge about the area around the hive, they have been subjects in important studies of cognitive

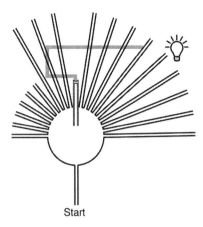

Start

FIGURE **3.3.** Setup used by Tolman, Ritchie, and Kalish (1946) to test place learning in rats. For training, only the pale gray alley was used. Rats learned to run from the start to the goal in the upper right, near the light; for testing, this alley was replaced with the "sunburst."

mapping. Behavior in the earliest of these, as in Tolman's rats, was no more than approach to cues near the goal (Dyer, 1991), but a later study (Menzel et al., 2005) is free of this problem. Bees accustomed to fly between their hive and a fixed food source were captured as they started home with nectar, quickly fitted with tiny radar antennas, and released several hundred meters away. They flew off in the compass direction they were headed when captured, but once they had gone about the distance normally needed to reach the hive, they began to fly around as if searching for it until they abruptly headed straight for the hive. This "searching flight" suggests bees do not have an exhaustive map of the area around the feeder—otherwise a "searching flight" would not be necessary—but rather a vector map incorporating distance and direction to the hive from discrete nearby points. Evidently they do not call on this spatial knowledge when traveling a well-known route between the hive and a familiar feeder but simply fly the learned distance and direction.

Many vertebrates such as monkeys, meerkats, and small rodents have been followed extensively while traveling around their home ranges, but here the nature of the animals' spatial knowledge can be hard to infer or manipulate (Janson & Byrne, 2007). Modern tracking devices have facilitated experiments with free-flying homing pigeons (Nagy, Akos, Biro, &

Vicsek, 2010). As such devices become smaller and more sophisticated we can look forward to a wealth of new information about spatial behavior in natural environments. But what about people? *Cognitive map* is an anthropomorphic concept, but people do not always seem to have them in the sense of an integrated representation of local space. Students tested in a classroom may not accurately indicate directions to other places on campus (Wang & Brockmole, 2003) nor even accurately relate a location inside a semienclosed booth to the surrounding room (Gibson, 2001). Many contemporary studies of human spatial learning test people "navigating" in virtual reality landscapes as in a video game (e.g., Doeller & Burgess, 2008). Virtual reality navigation has become a prominent tool in studies of human spatial cognition despite being largely egocentric and view based, lacking cues such as proprioceptive or vestibular feedback from self-propelled motion.

Concluding Remarks

The theme of this section is captured by the title of Mackintosh's (2002) review of animal spatial learning: "Do not ask whether they have a cognitive map but how they find their way about." In future sections of this book we will see other cases in which analysis in terms of elementary processes of learning and behavioral control is more illuminating than seeking evidence for grand but vaguely defined anthropomorphic processes. Also looking ahead at bigger themes, the elementary processes that contribute to navigation—not only the geometric module but also dead reckoning, landmark use, and so on—are some of the first clear examples in this book of modularity in cognition, in that they take distinct kinds of input and process it in distinctive ways (see also Jeffery, 2010). As we have seen, human children and adults share these functional modules, although special treatments such as disorientation or blindfolding may be needed to bring them out. In addition, uniquely among animals, adult humans can use maps and spatial language (Landau & Lakusta, 2009). This theme of shared modular systems alongside of human-unique processes will reappear. It is developed further in Chapter 5.

Two Timing Systems

Animals have two systems for representing and responding to time. The circadian system, present even in bacteria and plants, synchronizes activity with local day and night. The interval timing system, in vertebrates and some invertebrates, represents intervals of arbitrary durations from seconds to minutes and hours. Both play a role in learning and memory. Although one current model embraces both systems, there are crucial differences between them.

Circadian Timing

A universal adaptation to the daily alternation of light and darkness is a daily rhythm of activity and rest (Dunlap, Loros, & Decoursey, 2003). Such rhythms continue in constant light or darkness, showing they are not a direct response to the environment. However, the free-running or *endogenous* rhythms are generally slightly shorter or longer than 24 hours, that is, *circa* a day, hence *circadian*. A short daily pulse of light or dark at the right phase of the free-running cycle can be enough to resynchronize it to 24 hours, an example of *entrainment*. Circadian rhythms can be entrained only to periods of around 24 hours, with species-characteristic limits, and only by light and other species-characteristic events.

Circadian rhythms allow animals to do the best thing at each time of day, sometimes through learning, possibly because the time of day when things happen is encoded automatically along with their other features (Gallistel, 1990; but see Thorpe & Wilkie, 2006). For example, honeybees learn to visit flowers when they have the most nectar. Such time-place learning is demonstrated in the laboratory by training animals to visit a different feeder at each time of day. When subjects are then entrained to a shifted light-dark cycle, their choices shift along with their circadian rhythm.

Interval Timing

Although durations of events are important in all sorts of learning and memory, most studies of how animals time intervals shorter than a day employ instrumental conditioning (see Church, 2002). For example, in the frequently used *peak procedure* the first response a fixed time after a signal comes on is reinforced. In occasional *empty trials* no reinforcement is given, and the signal lasts much longer than usual. Although only one response is required, animals typically make many more, at a rate rising to a peak at about the time of reinforcement and falling again on empty trials (Fig. 3.4). This pattern of errors is the same whether the interval being timed is seconds, minutes, or hours, with a width proportional to that interval. Hence, closely similar curves result from rescaling the data as in Figure 3.4. This property, referred to as *scalar timing*, is an instance of *Weber's Law*, which applies to perception of magnitudes in general. In systems obeying Weber's Law, large quantities are discriminated proportionately as precisely as small ones. For instance, 40 seconds is discriminated from 30 seconds about as well as 4 seconds is discriminated from 3 seconds. Numerous species tested in various timing paradigms show data consistent with it. In the laboratory, lights, tones, intertrial intervals, and lengths of experimental sessions all may be timed, sometimes concurrently. In the field, hummingbirds simultaneously track the rates at which nectar repletes in two kinds of flowers (Henderson, Hurly, Bateson, & Healy, 2006). Thus, unlike circadian timing, interval timing is used with arbitrary events of arbitrary durations.

A second noteworthy property of interval timing is revealed in *temporal bisection*, a procedure for discovering the duration perceived as halfway between two training durations. For instance, a rat trained to choose one lever after a 3-second tone and another lever after a

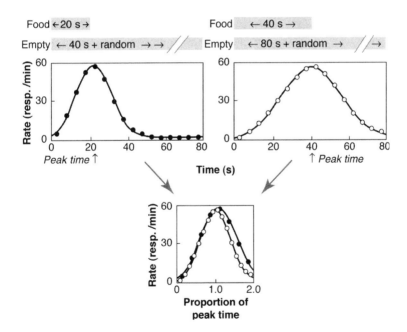

FIGURE **3.4.** Average data from rats trained in the peak procedure with reinforcement 20 or 40 seconds after the beginning of the interval on food trials; no food was given on empty trials. The lower part of the figure shows such data superimposed by rescaling the x-axis. Redrawn from S. Roberts (1981) with permission.

12-second tone has unrewarded test trials with tones of intermediate durations. The duration at which the two levers are chosen equally often—the psychological middle—is not 7.5 seconds, halfway between 3 and 12, their arithmetic mean, but 6 seconds, their geometric mean (the square root of 3 times 12). In the model discussed next, this finding implies that although the perception of time grows linearly with actual duration, durations are compared as ratios (e.g., 6 is the midpoint of 3 and 12 because 6:3 = 12:6).

Models of Interval Timing

The most influential theory of interval timing is the information-processing, pacemaker-accumulator, or *Scalar Expectancy (SET)* model (Gibbon & Church, 1990) in which timing is based on a hypothetical pacemaker that emits pulses at a constant but fairly fast rate. Onset of an interesting event switches these pulses into an accumulator, a counter in working memory. The final count for an event is stored in reference memory, which is not an average but a record of all relevant accumulator values (Gibbon, Church, Fairhurst, & Kacelnik, 1988). When timing a familiar signal, the total in the accumulator is compared to a sample from the reference memory; if their ratio exceeds some threshold, the animal makes an appropriate response. Because the pacemaker rate fluctuates randomly, total pulses will vary more when longer intervals are timed, accounting for the Weber's Law pattern of errors.

SET exemplifies a kind of information-processing model that has served cognitive psychology well, but it rests on largely hypothetical structures and processes. This disadvantage is not shared by the *oscillator model* (Buhusi & Meck, 2005; Gallistel, 1990). Animal nervous systems encode many oscillatory processes such as flapping or licking. The oscillator model assumes interval timing is the product of a system of such oscillators with a range of periodicities from very short to days or more. A time is encoded as the status of multiple oscillators. Multiple oscillators are necessary to make the readings unambiguous and precise. For example, with a circadian oscillator alone, 10 a.m. on one day is the same as 10 a.m. on any other day, and intervals of a few seconds involve only tiny changes in state. The model does not specify the frequencies of the hypothetical oscillators other than that one is circadian, but it does correctly predict that some intervals, interpreted as those close to an oscillator frequency, are discriminated especially sharply (Crystal, 2006).

A completely different approach to timing is represented by the behavioral theory of timing or Learning to Time (LeT) model (Machado,

1997), which accounts for interval timing without a clock, or indeed any internal cognitive structure at all. It derives from observations that when animals are fed at regular short intervals, on a *fixed time schedule*, regular sequences of behavior develop during interfood intervals. In terms of this model, such a sequence represents a sequence of motivational or behavioral states. In instrumental timing tasks, particular responses are conditioned to particular states, and these states succeed each other more rapidly at higher rates of food delivery. The latter assumption leads to the unique (and correct) prediction that how a given interval is timed depends on the context of other interfood intervals (Machado & Pata, 2005).

In summary, research on circadian and interval timing provides outstanding examples of precise and orderly data as well as important information about processes that inform many aspects of behavior. At present SET probably accounts best for the basic findings in the area, but the oscillator model and LeT each account best for a few others. Several other models of interval timing have been suggested (see Church, 2006). The oscillator model is the only one to encompass circadian and interval timing in one system, but it does so without explaining the special properties of the circadian system.

Numerical Cognition

"Can animals count?" is one of the oldest questions in comparative psychology. Well-known evidence suggesting they can comes from Clever Hans, the early twentieth-century horse who answered questions about numbers by tapping with his hoof (Pfungst, 1965). Hans *was* clever, not at arithmetic but at learning to respond to slight unconscious movements of questioners who knew the answers. Thus, he is remembered now mainly for this "Clever Hans effect," which remains something to guard against whenever experimenters interact directly with animal subjects.

The twentieth century saw many more attempts to teach animals counting-like skills (see Shettleworth, 1998). However, it gradually became clear that laboriously training animals to make arbitrary responses to limited small sets of items, for instance, to discriminate two from three rewards, does not capture a fundamental and phylogenetically widespread capacity to discriminate among sets of all sizes, albeit imprecisely. Coordinated research by comparative and developmental psychologists shows that this approximate number system is present in many species of animals and in humans of all ages, and we know a great deal about its basis in the brain (Nieder & Dehaene, 2009). Precise discrimination among numbers up to three or four is afforded by a second system, the object tracking system, present at least in primates, including infant humans. Like the approximate number system, it is employed spontaneously whenever relevant numbers of interesting things are present.

The Precise Small Number System

The properties of the precise small number system are illustrated by a study (Hauser, Carey, & Hauser, 2000) in which free-ranging rhesus macaques watched people place apple slices into each of two boxes. One box might have two slices, the other three. The experimenters stepped back and allowed a monkey to grab the contents of one box. The monkeys, which had not been trained in this task and each of which participated in only one trial, overwhelmingly chose the box with more apple pieces, but only if neither box had more than four items. For instance, they chose four over three but chose randomly with five versus three. Controls equating total items in the boxes by adding rocks to one showed the monkeys were attending to numbers of food items, not some correlate such as time spent putting things into a box. Babies show the same pattern in parallel studies, but the set size limit for precise discrimination is three for babies younger than about a year. Related studies have exploited the fact that babies and monkeys look longer at unexpected than expected events to demonstrate a kind of implicit arithmetic (Cordes & Brannon, 2008). For instance, monkeys saw one eggplant and then a second placed behind a screen. If raising the screen then revealed only one eggplant, they looked longer than if it revealed two, as if they computed "1 + 1 = 2" and were puzzled to see a different result.

All these effects are explained as output of the object file system, a limited-capacity perceptual memory responsible for identifying and tracking objects as individuals with unique spatiotemporal addresses. Sets are compared by one-to-one matching of these temporary "object files" in short-term memory. The two signatures of object tracking as a system of numerosity discrimination are limited capacity (sets of at most four even in human adults) and precision within those limits, such that, for instance, two versus three is discriminated as well as one versus two. The second fundamental system differs in both respects.

The Approximate Number System

The features of the approximate number system are well illustrated by a study in which rhesus macaques were trained to respond to two displays on a touchscreen in order of the number of items they contained. As indicated in Figure 3.5, the sizes and arrangements of items and the sizes of backgrounds varied from trial to trial, so cues normally correlated with a number such as area covered did not predict reward. The monkeys began the task with sets of 1–9 items. Once they were performing well, they received occasional unrewarded trials with up to 30 items. Performance remained well above chance even when both numerosities were novel (e.g., 20 vs. 30), evidence for a concept of relative numerosity, something like "less" versus "more." The data in the figure come from trials with all pairs of even numbers between 2 and 30 as a function of their ratio. Notice that unlike the case with the small number system or verbal counting, discrimination is often far from perfect. The importance of ratio to accuracy is a characteristic of systems obeying Weber's Law. The pattern of error as a function of ratio implies two other key features of Weber's Law, a distance and a magnitude effect. Numerosities are better discriminated the greater the distance between them, but a given absolute difference is better discriminated the smaller the magnitudes involved. Thus accuracy with 5 versus 10 is less than with 5 versus 20 but about the same as with 15 versus 30. Like durations, numerical magnitudes are bisected at their geometric mean, again consistent with Weber's Law.

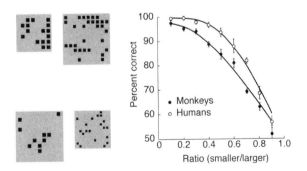

FIGURE **3.5.** (*Left*) Examples of displays for testing sensitivity to numerosity with other features controlled. Density (% of surface covered) is equated in the top pair of panels, total perimeter of items in the lower pair. Monkeys and people had to touch first the smaller and then the larger numerosity of a pair. (*Right*) Proportions of correct responses as a function of the ratio of the smaller to the larger numerosity. Redrawn from Cantlon and Brannon (2006) with permission.

Evidence for the approximate number system has been obtained with other nonhuman primates and with rats, pigeons, and human babies and with both successive and simultaneous stimuli. Babies are typically tested with habituation to visual items or trains of sounds. Human adults perform like other animals only when verbal counting is precluded, as by very brief display of the relatively large sets of items in Figure 3.5. Importantly, adults from a Brazilian tribe whose precise number language goes only to three or four performed no differently from numerate French controls in tests tapping the precise small number system or the approximate number system with large numbers. However, they fell below the French when precise counting of quantities above four was called for (Pica, Lemer, Izard, & Dehaene, 2004).

One theory of animal numerosity discrimination posits a system like the pacemaker-accumulator system for timing (Meck & Church, 1983). Other theories have been proposed (Nieder & Dehaene, 2009), but all assume an underlying analog representation of magnitude, that is, an implicit mental scale in which magnitudes are represented in order of size. Single-cell recordings from the brains of monkeys while they perform tasks like that illustrated in Figure 3.5 are revealing the neural basis of this representation (Nieder & Dehaene, 2009). Increasing evidence indicates that other dimensions varying in magnitude such as size, loudness, and time share the same analog magnitude scale, while also having some specificity (Cantlon, Platt, & Brannon, 2009; Kadosh, Lammertyn, & Izard, 2008). Evidence for a common representation includes the *semantic congruity effect*, the observation that people judge which of two animals is smaller more quickly than they judge which is larger if both animals are small, and vice versa for two large animals. Rhesus macaques show an analogous effect when comparing sizes of sets like those in Figure 3.5 (Cantlon et al., 2009).

Serial Order and Transitive Inference

Analog magnitude representation may extend to abstract content, as with arbitrary items that have acquired different values through training. The richest evidence comes from rhesus monkeys trained on *simultaneous chaining* (Terrace, 2006). In this procedure animals learn to contact images on a touchscreen in a fixed order. The images change position from trial to trial, so subjects cannot memorize a sequence of motor responses. Evidence that each image is identified with a position in an ordered mental list comes from experiments in which monkeys trained with several four-item lists were exposed to new lists with the old items reassorted. They learned the new lists much faster when items retained their original list positions than otherwise. Pigeons can also (slowly) learn lists of up to five items, but unlike monkeys, when required to order pairs of items they succeed only when the first or last item is included, as if using stimulus-specific rules such as "respond first to A" (Terrace, 2001). However, this may partly reflect a species difference in sensitivity to the change between training and test, that is, to a (literal) contextual variable (Chapter 2). With repeated reinforced trials on pairs of familiar items pigeons show evidence of representing their order in the original list (Scarf & Colombo, 2010).

In the world outside the laboratory, individuals in social groups may be ordered by dominance ranks (Chapter 4). For instance, if A always defeats B in contests and B always defeats C, it can be inferred that A will defeat C before seeing them meet. Such reasoning about dominance corresponds to *transitive inference* in human reasoning, and it was first studied as such in monkeys. The stimuli were arbitrary pairs of colors from which a linear relationship could be inferred. Animals were first trained with four pairs defining a five-item sequence, A+ B−, B+ C−, C+ D−, D+ E− where + means rewarded when an item appears with the given second (unrewarded) item. Then they were tested with the novel pair B and D. Note that B and D are each sometimes rewarded and sometimes nonrewarded during training, so choice of B over D (the observed outcome) could presumably result only from representing the items as an ordered sequence. Moreover, when monkeys learn three five-item sequences and then learn an ordered relationship between the last item of one sequence and the first of another, they spontaneously rank other items as if representing them in a single 15-item list (Treichler, Raghanti, & Van Tilburg, 2003).

Pigeons taught a single five-item sequence also choose B over D, but their performance reflects subtle aspects of the associative histories of B and D (see Chapter 10 in Shettleworth, 2010a). Primary among possible associative influences is *value transfer* (Zentall, Sherburne, Roper, & Kraemer, 1996). This refers to the observation that a stimulus can acquire value from other stimuli with which it is presented. In transitive inference training, B gains value on trials when it appears with A, which is always rewarded, whereas D loses value when it appears with the never-rewarded E. When people are given transitive inference problems like those for the monkeys and pigeons, that is, with nonsense symbols rather than meaningful material, they use either associative strength or reasoning, depending on how the problems are presented (Frank, Rudy, Levy, & O'Reily, 2005).

That the difference between monkeys and pigeons in these studies is not necessarily a difference between primates and birds is shown by studies in which pinyon jays (Paz-y-Mino, Bond, Kamil, & Balda, 2004) and cichlid fish (Grosenick, Clement, & Fernald, 2007) learned relative ranks of conspecifics by watching them in staged encounters. The subject jays watched as a stranger both lost a conflict over a peanut with a second stranger and won an encounter with a familiar bird dominant to the subject itself. Such subjects behaved more submissively toward the first stranger when they met than did control jays. Since pinyon jays, like rhesus monkeys, live in groups with stable dominance hierarchies whereas pigeons do not, this finding is consistent with the possibility that transitive inference ability is better developed in species that need it in social life. Further evidence comes from comparisons of performance in operant transitive inference tasks by pinyon jays and three less social corvid species (Bond, Wei, & Kamil, 2010).

Concluding Remarks

In the last decade or so, interest in the sweeping anthropomorphic yes-or-no question, "Can animals count?" has been replaced by an appreciation that numerical cognition has a few simple core components. Approximate numerosity discrimination and object tracking are evident in a variety of nonhuman species as well as in young children. How either or both of these systems contribute to development of the sophisticated numerical competence typical of educated human adults is the topic of ongoing research (see Chapter 5 and Carey, 2009; Leslie, Gelman, & Gallistel, 2008). What is clear is that these core systems are not replaced during development by uniquely human mathematical skills but exist alongside them and can be evoked by appropriate nonverbal materials.

Putting It Together: Foraging and Planning

Optimal Foraging Theory

Optimal Foraging Theory (OFT) is the area of behavioral ecology concerned with how aspects of foraging such as choosing food items or places to search for them (foraging *patches*) influence fitness, using mathematical models to predict the behavior that maximizes fitness. Thus, OFT takes a functional approach to behavior, but because many experiments designed to test it involve variables such as relative amounts of food, their locations, or times required to obtain them, understanding their results often requires understanding aspects of numerical, spatial, or temporal cognition. As a very simple example, if berries on Bush A are closer together than those on nearby B, A is the better place to forage. However, A may not be chosen consistently because foragers may need to learn the average time to find a berry in each bush. Learning is not instantaneous, and time is perceived and remembered with error. Thus, although data often match trends predicted by models of optimal foraging, the matches are rarely exact. Mechanistic analyses incorporating facts about perception, memory, and learning often account for the deviations (Stephens, Brown, & Ydenberg, 2007).

To take a more interesting example, at first glance it seems that two patches providing food at equal average rates should be chosen equally over the long run. One example of this situation in traditional studies of reinforcement is choice between fixed- and variable-interval (FI and VI) schedules. For example, responding on FI 20 s pays off every 20 seconds, whereas responding on VI 20 s pays off unpredictably at intervals averaging 20 seconds. Animals strongly prefer the VI, and the scalar expectancy theory of timing explains why (Gibbon et al., 1988). If memory for time is described by Weber's Law and if times are averaged by sampling from stored memories of all remembered intervals, samples from the VI will be skewed toward more precisely remembered short—preferred—intervals. Preference for a variable over a fixed option is referred to as *risk proneness*; preference for the fixed option is *risk aversion*. There are many conditions in which preferences should be influenced by variability, not only means. For example, an option that pays off at variable times may yield food before night falls when a fixed one will not.

When errors in learning, memory, or perception prevent behavior from being perfectly optimal, psychological mechanisms are said to be constraints on optimization. Some such constraints initially seem irrational or counterintuitive. Psychological experiments on self-control provide an excellent example. As in the choice between a rich piece of chocolate cake now and a healthy heart later in life, tests of self-control require subjects to choose between obtaining a comparatively small reward after a comparatively short delay and a larger reward after a longer delay. Most species that have been tested, including people, strongly prefer a short/small option (W. A. Roberts, 2002). For example, pigeons choose two food pellets delayed 2 seconds over six food pellets delayed 6 seconds even when the delay between reward and the next trial (the ITI) is arranged so all trials are equally long. For instance, the ITI might be 8 seconds after a two-pellet choice and 4 seconds after a six-pellet choice so that trials last 10 seconds no matter what the animal chooses.

Here consistent choice of two pellets gives only one-third the rate of food intake possible with consistent choice of the six-pellet option.

The mechanism underlying such suboptimal choice, also known as *impulsiveness*, *preference for immediacy*, or *temporal myopia*, is *delay discounting*, that is, the psychological value of a reward is discounted or diminished the longer it is delayed. In effect, at least in self-control-like situations, animals do not plan very far into the future, a point we return to presently. Is delay discounting a violation of optimality, or is it perhaps optimal in natural contexts? One possibility is that devaluing rewards that are not immediately available is an adaptation to an uncertain world (see also Stephens, Kerr, & Fernández-Juricic, 2004). A bird in the hand may well be worth two in the proverbial bush if the two in the bush fly away or are eaten by a competitor before one finds them. If preference for immediacy is adaptive, it should vary with species and circumstances such as hunger level or type of reward, as it does to some extent (e.g., Rosati, Stevens, Hare, & Hauser, 2007).

Economic Decision Making

At the same time as research connecting functional and psychological approaches to foraging has become increasingly sophisticated (e.g., Shapiro, Siller, & Kacelnik, 2008), related research on cognitive aspects of economic decision making has taken off with comparative behavioral studies and the development of *neuroeconomics*, the study of how value is represented in the brain (Glimcher & Rustichini, 2004). Economic theory resembles foraging theory in dealing with maximization, but whereas in foraging theory the currency to be maximized is fitness (i.e., representation of one's genes in future generations) or some variable presumed closely tied to fitness, the fundamental currency in economics is *utility*, or subjective value. Still, since evolution would be expected to produce creatures that value whatever contributes most to fitness, these two approaches should ultimately come to the same thing.

Just as in foraging, in the situations of interest to economists people and other animals do not always make the intuitively most rational or optimal decisions, and considerable research has been devoted to understanding why (Kacelnik, 2006; Santos & Hughes, 2009; Todd & Gigerenzer, 2007). One example is the *sunk costs effect*, in which a goal is overvalued simply because one has already put effort into trying to obtain it. In psychology, this phenomenon is explained in terms of cognitive dissonance. However, recent comparative studies suggest that it reflects a species-general mechanism in which the value of a reward is remembered in terms not of its intrinsic qualities but of how it was experienced. For example, starlings (Marsh, Schuck-Paim, & Kacelnik, 2004) and desert locusts (Pompilio, Kacelnik, & Behmer, 2006) remember food experienced when very hungry as more valuable than the same food experienced when sated. Because starlings and locusts sense hunger through different mechanisms, this research also provides a rare illustration of how functionally similar effects can be produced by very different mechanisms in unrelated species.

To demonstrate the importance of relative value, animals are typically trained in two separate situations. Cue A is associated with the item in question in one situation (say, when very hungry pecking a red key yields five food pellets) and cue B in the other (when sated, pecking green yields five food pellets). A and B are then presented in some intermediate test situation, here moderate hunger. A is preferred even when, paradoxically, independent evidence shows the animal knows the absolute values of A and B do not differ (Pompilio & Kacelnik, 2010). This is but one example of how experience determines the psychological value of rewards for both humans (Santos & Hughes, 2009) and other animals (Dickinson & Balleine, 2002).

Mental Time Travel: Do Animals Plan Ahead?

Experiments on self-control show that animals are not very good at planning even only a few seconds or minutes ahead. And many untrained future-oriented behaviors such as hoarding, migrating, or nest building are performed without planning, in that they occur in young animals that have not yet experienced their consequences. The fact that a person heading south for the winter or furnishing a nursery for an expected baby can "mentally time travel" to the anticipated future event need not mean that other animals performing analogous behaviors are doing the same. Indeed, because animals are so well equipped with ways to prepare for the future without representing it as such (Raby & Clayton, 2009; W. A. Roberts, 2002), the possibility that any animals do think about the future and make plans was not seriously entertained until relatively recently.

The stimulus for attempting to test whether animals do engage in mental time travel was a prominent claim (Suddendorf & Corballis, 1997) that they do not, that animals are cognitively stuck in the present, a claim dubbed the *Bischof-Kohler hypothesis*, after its originators. In addition, cognitive neuroscientists became interested in the connection between episodic memory, which in humans involves mental time travel into the past (Chapter 2), and imagining the future. Human episodic memory presumably evolved partly because it facilitates imagining future scenarios, consistent with overlap between the brain areas involved in episodic memory and planning (Addis, Wong, & Schacter, 2007). Evidence for episodic-like memory in other species (Chapter 2) thus encourages the search for evidence that they also plan.

Criteria for behavioral evidence of planning are still evolving (e.g., W. A. Roberts & Feeney, 2009). Their acceptability often relies more on folk psychology than on functional similarity to any experimental evidence for humans. Suddendorf and Busby (2005) proposed that planning-like behavior must be novel and it must be performed in the service of a motivational state other than the one the animal is in currently. The first criterion rules out species-typical future-oriented behaviors such as migration. Both rule out responses learned for delayed reinforcement, as does a requirement that the behavior be shown as soon as the relevant information is provided. A further requirement for genuinely humanlike planning is that it be expressed in more than one functional domain. We can plan for everything from today's lunch to next year's summer holiday, but so far there is no evidence that other animals can plan for more than at most one thing.

In one of the first candidate demonstrations of animal planning (Raby, Alexis, Dickinson, & Clayton, 2007), Western scrub jays learned that they would have breakfast in one "room" of a cage and not in another (Fig. 3.6). When then allowed to cache food in the evening, they cached more in the "no breakfast" room, as if anticipating it would be most needed there. Similarly, when peanuts had been provided for breakfast on one room and dog kibble in the other, in the evening the birds tended to cache more of the alternative food in each room. Importantly, the data in each of these experiments come from a single test, before the consequences of specific choices could be learned. However, the birds may have been expressing a natural propensity to spread out caches of a given type, and this has not been tested (see W. A. Roberts & Feeney, 2009).

A further study with scrub jays (Correia, Dickinson, & Clayton, 2007) opposed current and future values of peanuts and kibble. Both could be cached, but because the birds had just been satiated on one, they treated it as relatively low in value and cached more of the other. Then the food that had *not* been devalued during caching was devalued at the time of recovery. After one such experience, the birds switched toward caching the currently devalued item, as if foreseeing its future increase in value. Similarly, black-capped chickadees, another food-storing species, learned to forage for relatively low-valued seeds when doing so increased

Caching tray	Food bowl	Caching tray

FIGURE **3.6.** Diagram (not to scale) of the setup used by Raby et al. (2007) to test planning in scrub jays. Seeds were in the food bowl and the caching trays present in the end "rooms" in the evening only for the final test. Otherwise the birds ate uncachable powdered food from the food bowl in the evening and were then closed into one room or the other for the night, where they either had breakfast or not the next morning, depending on the room. After Raby et al. (2007) with permission.

the number of high-valued worms available elsewhere 30 minutes later (Feeney, Roberts, & Sherry, 2011).

Even if these findings hold up to further scrutiny (see Suddendorf & Corballis, 2008b), do they necessarily mean that when choosing an action, animals are "mentally time traveling" to its imagined future outcome and reasoning that performing that action will lead to the outcome? Recall from Chapter 2 that flexible performance of an instrumental response is jointly determined by knowledge that the response leads to a given outcome (the response-outcome association) and desire for that outcome (Dickinson, 2008). In these terms, mental time travel implies that at the time of choosing an action the response-outcome association retrieves an episodic memory of that action's past outcome. For instance, after the first trial in the study of Correia et al., the birds cached peanuts when sated because they remembered retrieving desirable peanuts and anticipated doing so again. But the associative structure of instrumental behavior permits an alternative account, dubbed by Dickinson (2011) Mnemonic Associative Theory, that does not involve thinking about the future. On this account, an action is recalled at the time its outcome is experienced, and as generally true in conditioning, simultaneous activation of representations (here, action and outcome) strengthens the association between them. Thus, recovering peanuts reminds the birds of caching them. Because peanuts are now desirable, caching peanuts automatically becomes more strongly associated with the (remembered) caching situation, causing the birds to cache more of them next time they are in that situation, but not because they imagine desiring peanuts in the future.

Mnemonic Associative Theory accounts for the results of "planning" experiments involving repeated trials of the same or similar types, including several in which apes chose tools for future use. For instance, chimpanzees and orangutans learned to use a tool to obtain grapes from a dispenser. On test trials the dispenser was disabled and suitable tools and other objects placed nearby (Mulcahy & Call, 2006). The apes could take the tools to an adjoining cage, where they were confined for an hour before renewed access to the dispenser. Planning here means taking the appropriate tool and bringing it back when the dispenser is again available. Most apes did this sometimes, but not in the consistent pattern indicative of understanding the need to plan. In a related study (Osvath & Osvath, 2008) chimpanzees and orangutans chose a hose that could later be used to drink fruit soup, sometimes preferring the hose to a grape that could be eaten immediately. After many successful trials with the hose, they chose novel tube-like objects over other novel objects, an effect explicable as generalization and/or learning the affordance (use) of such objects (Suddendorf, Corballis, & Collier-Baker, 2009).

One suggestion (W. A. Roberts & Feeney, 2009) is that genuine planning involves discriminating among different future times, in effect choosing an action depending on the task anticipated. Demonstrating planning in this sense would require training with cues predicting which task is coming next, making it a normal conditional discrimination (Chapter 2). Other approaches to future time travel have been suggested (e.g., Eichenbaum & Fortin, 2009; Zentall, 2010). Outside the lab, some have tried to test whether free-ranging animals choose foraging routes in a way that reflects knowledge of current food availability (Janson & Byrne, 2007).

In any case, although the Bischof-Kohler hypothesis may not (yet) have been conclusively contradicted, it has stimulated new understanding of the nature and variety of future-oriented behaviors in animals (Raby & Clayton, 2009). And as with issues such as insight (next section) or theory of mind (Chapter 4), attempts to document in animals processes based on human introspection both challenge researchers to specify what acceptable evidence from nonverbal creatures would be and reveal how much sophisticated behavior can be accomplished by "simpler" processes than those assumed in folk psychology.

Using Tools

Tool use and manufacture were traditionally seen as uniquely human, but they appear on many branches of the evolutionary tree (Bentley-Condit & Smith, 2010; Shumaker, Walkup, & Beck, 2011). Indeed, as described in Chapter 1, some birds use tools similarly to chimpanzees. Animal tool use was discussed in Chapter 1 to illustrate the integration of multiple approaches and methods in twenty-first-century comparative cognition research. Tool use by New Caledonian crows provided a case study in key issues, including anthropomorphism, Morgan's Canon, and the idea of animal intelligence.

As studies of the crows illustrate, contemporary research on animal tool use ranges from field work to laboratory experiments (Seed & Byrne, 2010). It addresses three central questions about cognition: To what extent does tool use imply physical causal understanding? Is insight ever involved? To what extent is tool use acquired via social learning? The first two are discussed in this chapter, the third in Chapter 4. But first, what exactly is a tool? A useful rough and ready definition was provided by Jane Goodall: "the use of an external object as a functional extension of mouth, beak, hand or claw in the attainment of an immediate goal (van Lawick-Goodall, 1971, p. 195)." Continuing debates about this and other definitions (Bentley-Condit & Smith, 2010; Shumaker et al., 2011) highlight the arbitrariness of anthropocentric categorizations of animal behaviors. For example, on most views, cracking a nut involves tool use when a monkey pounds it with a rock but not when a bird drops it on a rock. Manipulating a twig is tool use when a woodpecker finch is obtaining food but maybe not when a zebra finch is building a nest (Hansell & Ruxton, 2008; Shumaker et al., 2011). As these examples suggest, tool use by any definition may not be a class of behaviors supported by distinctive cognitive mechanisms (Emery & Clayton, 2009b).

Animal Folk Physics?

On one view (Osiurak, Jarry, & LeGall, 2010), two interacting sets of cognitive processes underlie tool use. Procedural or affordance learning, that is, learning what actions to perform and/or what actions are supported by different kinds of objects, is present in humans and other animals. Technical reasoning or folk physics, that is, understanding how or why tools work, may be uniquely human (see also Penn et al., 2008). For example, the trap tube introduced in Chapter 1 (see Fig. 3.7, top) tests whether animals using a stick to extract food from a transparent tube

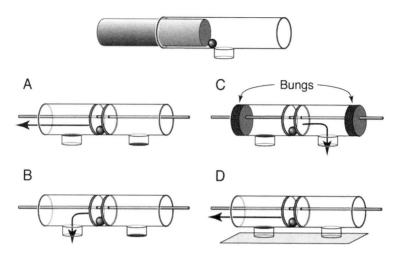

FIGURE **3.7.** (*Top*) Original trap tube design. Here the reward will be pushed out of the tube only if the stick tool is inserted from the right. Otherwise the reward will fall into the trap. (*Bottom*) Trap tubes presented to rooks by Seed et al. (2006) as described in the text. Tubes were on stands with the stick at beak height. In both *A* and *B*, pulling the stick to the left will release the reward. Tubes *C* and *D* each combine the "safe" ends of Tubes *A* and *B* but require pulling in opposite directions as indicated by the arrows. *A–D* after Seed et al. (2006) with permission.

understand what the tool does. Evidence that they do not is that primates and birds typically need to learn by trial and error to avoid a trap rather than doing so immediately. Moreover, when the trap is then rotated to the top so the stick can be inserted anywhere, they continue following a rule, as if not understanding the need for an unbroken surface, let alone anything about gravity.

A more powerful test involving traps and tubes first used for rooks (Seed, Tebbich, Emery, & Clayton, 2006) opposes physical understanding to transfer of learning based solely on perceptual cues. Because rooks do not naturally use tools, they had only to choose which end of a stick to pull. Birds trained initially on A (Fig. 3.7, bottom) succeeded immediately on B and vice versa, but this could reflect learning to pull away from the trap, which looked the same on both tubes. Physical understanding was tested by incorporating the "correct" ends of A and B in new configurations (C and D). Here, the two previously learned responses conflicted. Now only one of seven rooks transferred correct performance. Such exceptional performance by a single animal has been seen in related studies with apes and other species (Seed & Byrne, 2010), suggesting that a few individuals notice subtle perceptual cues and/or possess unusual conceptual abilities. In any case, this study is an example of how a series of transfer tasks can be used to distinguish among cognitive processes.

Related studies with apes make another important point: what to humans seem conceptually irrelevant differences in how tasks are presented can have profound effects on how animals solve them. Povinelli and colleagues (Povinelli, 2000) gave chimpanzees extensive tests in which the animals had to choose the one of two tools that would bring a treat within reach. For instance, in the "trap table" one of two identical rake-like implements would sweep food into a hole. Their controversial conclusion was that although the animals might gradually learn to choose effective tools, they showed no understanding of the unseen forces that make tools work. This conclusion may still stand, but it turns out that chimpanzees perform much better on apparently slight variations of trap table tasks. With a single rake to move into position—and thus no need to inhibit pulling the incorrect rake—they immediately avoid a hole (Girndt, Meier, & Call, 2008). When chimpanzees can use a finger to slide a reward out of an apparatus, they also succeed in avoiding traps, suggesting that attending to a tool interferes with processing other features of a task (Seed, Call, Emery, & Clayton, 2009). But human adults are not entirely rational when solving such tasks either. For instance, they avoid even harmless traps, as if perceptual biases override technical knowledge (Silva & Silva, 2006).

Tools have many properties not tested in tasks with traps, including material (e.g., floppy or stiff), size (e.g., length and thickness of sticks), and shape, that may be key for tools in nature. Studies of birds' and primates' ability to respond appropriately to variations in such properties generally show they discriminate the relevant perceptual cues very well (Seed & Byrne, 2010; Shettleworth, 2010a). Young children (Brown, 1990) and other animals (e.g., Hauser, Kralik, & Botto-Mahan, 1999) attend to functionally important properties of potential tools, for example, generalizing to novel tools on the basis of shape and ignoring color. However, the few relevant comparative studies provide no evidence as yet that species which use tools in nature excel at cognitive processes related to tool use (Emery & Clayton, 2009b; Seed & Byrne, 2010). Rather, youngsters' tendencies to manipulate objects in certain ways (see Chapter 1), together with general processes of social (Chapter 4) and/or trial-and-error learning, help to ensure that animals such as New Caledonian crows and chimpanzees develop into skilled adult tool users.

Insight

The classic observations suggesting that a process of insight underlies solution of novel tool-use problems come from Kohler's (1925/1959) studies of captive chimpanzees using sticks and stacking boxes to obtain otherwise inaccessible food. For instance, in the "banana and box problem," a banana hangs out of reach and a box suitable to climb on is nearby. Kohler reported that chimpanzees might begin by jumping at the banana and then perhaps stop and engage in some unrelated activity before suddenly moving the box under the banana and climbing up to grab it. To Kohler and other Gestalt psychologists, such behavior reflected *insight* or "seeing the solution," perceptual restructuring but not necessarily physical understanding. People intuitively identify their own insights by the accompanying feeling of surprise and delight, the "aha experience" (Kounios & Beeman, 2009). However, whether such solutions involve a process distinct from that underlying analytical solutions (i.e., mental trial and error) is debated. Subjectively insightful and analytical solutions are all facilitated by experience with the elements of a problem, suggesting a common mechanism (Weisberg, 2006).

Because we cannot ask animals about their aha experiences, research on animal insight has focused on novel solutions that seem to defy explanation in terms of past learning in appearing suddenly, not preceded by obvious trial and error. But because experience together with species-typical responses and the arrangement of present cues can influence behavior in subtle ways, investigating candidates for insight requires comparing groups of animals exposed to different experiences and/or test conditions. The best example of this approach is the demonstration that pigeons can solve the "banana and box problem" (Epstein, Kirshnit, Lanza, & Rubin, 1984). The successful birds had been rewarded separately for *(1)* climbing onto a box and pecking a toy banana and *(2)* pushing the box from various locations toward a spot on the wall, with the banana absent. When confronted with the box displaced from the now-inaccessible banana, they initially looked back and forth between them, appearing confused, but very soon began pushing the box toward the banana. Control birds given only one part of the initial training failed unless random pushing of the box moved it under the banana.

Such *interconnection* (Epstein, 1985), combining old behaviors in new ways, involves several well-defined processes. Apparent confusion resulted from the presence of cues for two conflicting behaviors: pushing and pecking. Pushing predominated because jumping at the inaccessible banana had previously been extinguished. The box was pushed toward the banana because, like the absent spot, it had been paired with food, that is, through mediated generalization (Chapter 2). And once the box was under the banana it provided a cue in the presence of which climbing had been strongly reinforced.

The recent upsurge of interest in animal tool behavior has led to numerous provocative observations inviting interpretation in terms of insight but few experimental analyses like that just outlined. This research includes both primates and birds (see Seed & Byrne, 2010). Here we look at examples from corvids, beginning with the famous Betty, the New Caledonian crow who made a wire hook (Weir, Chappell, & Kacelnik, 2002). Experienced using ready-made hooks to pull a little bucket of meat out of a transparent well, when only a straight wire was available she first tried to extract the bucket but then began poking the wire at the base of the well. One end became wedged there, and when she pulled up on the free end it bent into a hook, which she used to get the reward. Betty repeated roughly the same actions on further trials, but because these were reinforced only the first trial is relevant to the question of insight. It is easy to see how Betty's actions parallel those of the pigeons in the last paragraph, but more subjects and tests of the role of experience with hooks are clearly needed. In the wild, New Caledonian crows make hooked tools from sticks and leaves, but a predisposition to make tools may be unnecessary: non-tool-making corvids, rooks, experienced with wooden hooks, also made usable wire hooks (Bird & Emery, 2009).

More progress has been made with a task in which a stone dropped down a tube collapses a platform and releases food. Rooks (Bird & Emery, 2009) and New Caledonian crows (von Bayern, Heathcote, Rutz, & Kacelnik, 2009) trained to nudge the stone from the top of the tube brought stones to the tube themselves. But experience with stones in the apparatus was apparently not necessary: two New Caledonian crows that had used their beaks to push down the platform through a short tube then used stones with the long tube, and one did so after using a stick. Experience with beak or stick may have taught the birds the affordance of the platform, that is, that it could collapse to release food. Affordance learning can result from simply watching an apparatus operated remotely (Chapter 4), suggesting one way to extend this study. Or perhaps the birds learn that something has to contact the platform. Either way, the biggest unsolved mystery is why they then supply stones themselves.

One factor to consider in future attempts to solve this mystery is underlined by studies of *metatool* use by corvids. A metatool is a tool used to make or obtain another tool. From using a stone to sharpen another stone to modern manufacturing, metatool use is a key human activity, but it need not always involve uniquely human cognition. Interconnection may explain sequential use of two or more tools following training with each separately. For example, in several studies with New Caledonian crows, meat is in a hole, a stick long enough to access it is out of reach, but a short stick is nearby. Especially if use of the long stick has already been reinforced and use of the short stick extinguished (as in Taylor, Hunt, Holzhaider, & Gray, 2007) and if no other accessible tool is present, a natural propensity to manipulate sticks and stimulus generalization both predict using the short stick to access the more valuable long one. More informative is a study with multiple inaccessible tools and an unpredictable sequence of tasks such that a short accessible tool can sometimes be used directly to get reward and sometimes as a metatool. Experience using the beak to extract the longer tools from a container increased crows' use of the short tool to do so, but overall behavior was not adjusted to the task requirements in a way suggesting causal reasoning or planning (Wimpenny, Weir, Clayton, Rutz, & Kacelnik, 2009).

Concluding Remarks

Both in the laboratory and in their natural environments, animals use tools in remarkable ways. A chimpanzee bringing tools to a termite mound (Sanz, Morgan, & Gulick, 2004) or a New Caledonian crow extracting grubs from a tree trunk looks as if it understands what it is doing, but the preponderance of evidence indicates that such behavior results from more basic cognitive processes. Isolating candidates for other processes such as insight or causal understanding will require further critical studies imaginatively designed to deconstruct the tasks involved into their elements and test the role of experience with each one. However, it is important to bear in mind that although people possess folk physics or technical knowledge (Osiurak et al., 2010), they do not always use it in deciding what to do with tools. In tasks originally designed for other primates, human subjects display irrational biases (Silva & Silva, 2006) and undue control by the same perceptual factors as chimpanzees (Silva, Silva, Cover, Leslie, & Rubalcaba, 2008). When confronted with the "bucket and well" problem given Betty the crow, children younger than 5 years old do not spontaneously make a hook to pull the bucket out (Beck, Apperly, Chappell, Guthrie, & Cutting, 2011). Thus, the anthropomorphism inherent in many tests of animal tool behavior may not always be justified even for humans.

As with spatial and numerical cognition, comparative research on tool use is revealing a role for basic processes that we share with other species while highlighting the ways in which human cognition is unique (Shettleworth, 2010b). Thus, human adults have both procedural and technical knowledge (Osiurak et al., 2010), both the approximate number system and precise verbal counting, dead reckoning and the "geometric module" along with mapping and spatial language (Landau & Lakusta, 2009). We will see more evidence for this emerging theme in Chapter 4 and bring it all together in Chapter 5.

Suggestions for Further Reading

Cantlon, J. F., Platt, M. L., & Brannon, E. M. (2009). Beyond the number domain. *Trends in Cognitive Science*, *13*, 83–89.

Dickinson, A. (2011). Goal-directed behaviour and future planning in animals. In R. Menzel & J. Fischer (Eds.), *Animal Thinking: Contemporary Issues in Comparative Cognition* (pp. 79–91). Cambridge, MA: MIT Press.

Kacelnik, A. (2006). Meanings of rationality. In S. Hurley & M. Nudds (Eds.), *Rational Animals?* (pp. 87–106). Oxford, England: Oxford University Press.

Nieder, A., & Dehaene, S. (2009). Representation of number in the brain. *Annual Review of Neuroscience*, *32*, 185–208.

Penn, D. C., & Povinelli, D. J. (2007). Causal cognition in human and nonhuman animals: A comparative, critical review. *Annual Review of Psychology*, *58*, 97–118.

Roberts, W. A. (2002). Are animals stuck in time? *Psychological Bulletin*, *128*, 473–489.

Seed, A., & Byrne, R. (2010). Animal tool-use. *Current Biology*, *20*, R1032–R1039.

Shettleworth, S. J. (2010). Chapters 8–11 in *Cognition, Evolution, and Behavior* (2nd ed.). New York: Oxford University Press.

Shumaker, R.W., Walkup, C. R., & Beck, B. B. (Eds.). (2011). *Animal Tool Behavior* (Revised and updated ed.). Baltimore, MD: Johns Hopkins University Press.

Suddendorf, T., & Corballis, M. C. (2010). Behavioural evidence for mental time travel in nonhuman animals. *Behavioural Brain Research*, *215*, 292–298.

Terrace, H. S. (2006). The simultaneous chain: A new look at serially organized behavior. In E. A. Wasserman & T. R. Zentall (Eds.), *Comparative Cognition* (pp. 481–511). New York: Oxford University Press.

Wiener, J., Shettleworth, S. J., Bingman, V. P., Cheng, K., Healy, S., Jacobs, L. F., et al. (2011). Animal navigation: A synthesis. In R. Menzel & J. Fischer (Eds.), *Animal Thinking: Contemporary Issues in Comparative Cognition* (pp. 51–76). Cambridge, MA: MIT Press.

....

CHAPTER 4

Social Cognition

Social cognition refers to the processes unique to learning about and interacting with other individuals. Most often these are members of one's own species (*conspecifics*), but interactions with members of other species may involve the same mechanisms. Just because a situation is social it need not engage specifically social cognition. For example, many territorial male songbirds associate the songs of their neighbors with the location from which they are usually sung, and they attack if they hear a neighbor singing elsewhere. A change in location is a cue that the neighbor may be trying to take over new territory, so the behavior functions to defend the attacker's territorial boundaries. The mechanism is associative learning together with habituation (here, of aggressive behavior) to familiar configurations (Dong & Clayton, 2009), a social *use* of basic cognitive mechanisms rather than specifically social cognition.

This chapter has three main sections. First, the basics: what do animals know about their social companions and how do they come to know it? A central issue here is whether any animals have theory of mind. That is, do animals know anything about others' knowledge, beliefs, or other mental states, or do they respond to behavioral cues alone? Do species differ in this respect and how are any differences related to phylogeny, social system, and/or brain size? Next we address social learning. What and how do animals learn from each other? Do any animals imitate, and if so how is imitation possible? Can any animals be said to teach? Does social learning result in anything that could be called culture, or is culture unique to humans? Finally we look at the intrinsically social activity of communicating. Does emitting communicative signals imply understanding others' need for information, that is, theory of mind? What does animal communication have in common with human language?

Most of the questions in the preceding paragraph do not yet have clear answers. The study of social cognition is perhaps the fastest growing and most contentious area discussed in this book. The tension between explanations in terms of basic processes and those invoking mentalistic understanding, or folk psychology, is nowhere stronger than here. Many of the theoretical ideas reflect a traditional primatocentric approach, but this is gradually being overturned by increasing evidence that social behaviors of nonprimate mammals, some birds, and even fish may equal in complexity those of apes and monkeys.

Social Behavior: The Basics

Social Complexity and Social Knowledge

The relatively large brains of primates and their exceptional perfor-mance in laboratory tests of cognition have long been thought to reflect adaptations to the complex cognitive demands of social life (Byrne & Bates, 2010; Humphrey, 1976; Jolly, 1966). This *social theory of intel-lect* (or *social brain theory*) has considerable support, but there is also much to debate. For example, what measure of sociality should be cor-related with what aspect of brain size? Sheer group size does not insure high demands on cognition. In herds or flocks, anonymous individu-als may just follow rules about how to move relative to near neighbors (Couzin, 2009). The social brain hypothesis seems to assume general rather than modular intelligence, but unlike with hippocampus size and spatial memory in food-storing birds (Chapter 2), we know very little about the neural underpinnings of social cognition (Healy & Rowe, 2007; but see Lefebvre & Sol, 2008). Here, further comparative analysis of social behavior can develop hand in hand with neurobiology (Dunbar & Shultz, 2007).

The most interesting social cognition appears in species that form stable groups in which the members recognize each other as individu-als with differentiated social roles such as dominant-subordinate, pair-bonded, mother-offspring. Here the number of relationships that might be learned increases exponentially with group size, if nothing else increas-ing demands on memory. Each kind of relationship, perhaps simultane-ously with other relationships, predicts different behaviors. For instance, a baboon approaching an infant needs to know not only who its mother is but that mother's kinship and/or dominance relationships to itself. The mother's response may be modulated by recent events such as a fight between her relatives and those of the approaching baboon (Cheney & Seyfarth, 2007). But arguably some problems in the physical world equal social problems in complexity. One confronting some primates is tracking the availability of fruits in a tropical forest with hundreds of species ripening on different schedules, and indeed there is some evidence that the nature of species-typical foraging problems is correlated with brain measures (Byrne & Bates, 2010; Dunbar & Shultz, 2007). Nevertheless, there is a fundamental difference between the social and physical worlds, as reflected in the models in behavioral ecology. Optimality models are used in foraging theory (Chapter 3) because the environment can be assumed to change only as a result of the actor's behavior, but game theory is used to model social behavior, including social foraging, because here the best thing to do depends on what others are doing.

Much of what we know about animal social organization comes from studies in the field or with reasonably sized captive groups. Long-term observations can yield enough data to support causal inferences, for example, as to whether sheer spatial proximity or relationship best predicts mutual aid against aggressors (e.g., Silk, 1999), but experiments are most revealing. In one approach, hidden loudspeakers present sequences of vocalizations representing either familiar or unexpected social interactions between the subject's social companions (see Cheney & Seyfarth, 2007). Differences in the responses evoked, for example, looking longer toward a speaker playing an incongruous sequence such as a dominant animal vocalizing submissively toward a subordinate, reveal sensitivity to the social information involved.

Studies like those just sketched have revealed much about the social knowledge of primates and many other species (de Waal & Tyack, 2003; Emery, Clayton, & Frith, 2007), but experiments on captive animals are usually necessary to learn how such knowledge is acquired and what it consists of. The challenge here is controlling the behavioral events to be learned about. One way to address it is illustrated by the studies of social transitive inference described in Chapter 3 in which jays and fish watched staged interactions between live conspecifics. An approach permitting better control over characteristics of the stimulus animals is to splice audio (cf. McGregor, 2005) or video recordings to create artificial interactions. In one such study, rhesus macaques were trained to indicate the dominant one of two individuals in each of several short video clips. For instance, one monkey might be threatening and the other jumping away. They then generalized to scenes showing different individuals (Paxton et al., 2010), suggesting these monkeys have a social concept of dominance.

Elements of Social Cognition

A key ingredient of social cognition is implicit in the preceding discussion: animals know other individuals' relationships to each other, and they may learn about these *third-party relationships* by observing, or *eavesdropping* (cf. McGregor, 2005). At one time it appeared (Tomasello & Call, 1997) that sensitivity to third-party relationships set primates apart from other species, but it is now clear that this sensitivity is shared not only by nonprimate mammals (e.g., hyenas; Holekamp, Sakai, & Lundrigan, 2007) but also—as indicated by the transitive inference studies mentioned earlier—by some birds and fish. Exactly what knowledge of a third-party relationship consists of is a largely unanswered question. For example, primate kinship may be expressed by frequent mutual grooming, sitting close together, cooperating in aggressive interactions, among other ways. Are such multiple behaviors encoded in a unitary way, similar to the behavioral abstractions discussed later in this chapter in the context of theory of mind? What would representing sets of behavioral interactions as relationships have in common with representing physical categories (Chapter 2)? Are relationships encoded hierarchically, for example, as dominance relationships within families that themselves have dominance relationships (Bergman, Beehner, Cheney, & Seyfarth, 2003)?

Two very basic ingredients set social apart from physical cognition. First, living beings are distinctive in being animate, that is, moving on their own, and goal directed. Much evidence from human infants and some from other species indicates that simple cues to animacy engage a set of expectations peculiar to living beings. Even a cartoon of moving colored balls may be seen as a social interaction: if Red moves toward Green, which moves away as Red approaches, Red is perceived as chasing Green (Scholl & Tremoulet, 2000). Young children encode motion like that at the top of Figure 4.1 as that of something animate, looking longer at a test display inconsistent with goal directedness (the "old action test" in which the ball still jumps when the barrier is removed rather than taking the shortest path; Gergely, Nádasdy, Csibra, & Bíró, 1995). Recognition of animacy and goal directedness may be a foundation for more complex forms of social cognition (Gigerenzer, 1997; Spelke & Kinzler, 2007).

Second, animals have eyes, and where they are looking is a good cue to what they will do next or where important things are in the

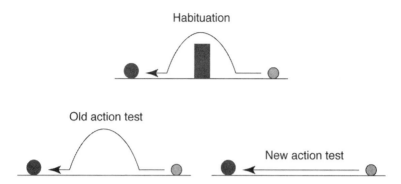

FIGURE **4.1.** Test for perception of intentionality. In each display, a single ball moves from the gray to the black position along the arrow. After habituation to the ball jumping over the barrier, the subject sees one of the lower displays. After Gergely et al. (1995) with permission.

environment. Accordingly, many mammals and birds are sensitive to the direction of other individuals' gaze. Apes, monkeys, goats, ibises, ravens, and others turn to look toward a distant location being gazed at by a human experimenter or conspecific (Byrne & Bates, 2010; Emery, 2000). But responding to gaze could be reflexive, in ethological terms a response to a sign stimulus. That is to say, importantly, *looking* or gazing is distinct from the mentalistic *seeing*: tracking gaze does not imply understanding others' experience of seeing. But what if an individual gazes toward a location you cannot see, for example at his side of a barrier placed between you? In such situations, apes, some monkeys (Amici, Aureli, Visalberghi, & Call, 2009), and ravens but not ibises (Loretto, Schloegl, & Bugnyar, 2010) move to look behind the barrier, as if aware their companion must be seeing something interesting. Even more strongly suggestive of this interpretation, if there is nothing behind, the barrier apes (but not monkeys; Amici et al., 2009) "check back," looking again at a human experimenter (Rosati & Hare, 2009). It could be argued that this behavior reveals an expectation of seeing something that is conditioned to the basic gaze-following response, but the species differences here seem more compatible with apes having an understanding of gaze that other species lack. However, if gaze following is an adaptation for social life, it is not clear why gaze-following skills of apes should be different from those of other highly social primates (Rosati & Hare, 2009).

Theory of Mind

Sensitivity to the gaze of others is but one component of *theory of mind*, the understanding that others have knowledge, beliefs, desires, and the like (intentional states; Dennett, 1983). This central concept in social cognition was introduced by Premack and Woodruff (1978) in an article titled "Does the chimpanzee have a theory of mind?" but it has been studied most in young children. A key test here is the *false belief task*: a child sees a toy hidden by the experimenter, say in a basket, while a stooge, say a clown, looks on. The clown leaves the scene and the experimenter moves the toy to a second hiding place, say a box. The clown returns and the child is asked, "Where will he look for the toy?" Up to the age of about 4 years (see Apperly & Butterfill, 2009) children say the ignorant stooge will look in the box, as if unable to distinguish another's beliefs from their own knowledge about the true state of the world. Older children, like adults, predict the stooge will search the original hiding place. Notice, however, that a correct prediction need not imply theory of mind but could be based on behavioral cues. That is, a child could explain her prediction by saying, "Because he was looking there when you hid it" rather than "Because that's where he thinks it is." The distinction between use of behavioral cues alone and inference about others' mental states based on such cues—or behavior reading versus mind reading—is the root of the many controversies and challenges surrounding attempts to answer Premack and Woodruff's question.

To date, no nonhuman animal has unambiguously passed any form of false belief test (Byrne & Bates, 2010; Call & Tomasello, 2008). More often used has been the simpler *object choice test*. Here subjects choose between two containers that might hide food. In the original version for chimpanzees (Fig. 4.2; Povinelli & Eddy, 1996), a knowledgeable companion, usually a person, points toward or looks at the baited container. In versions with competition, the companion can see or has seen the food in one location, whereas the subject knows food is in both. When both animals are allowed to get the food, the subject should avoid competition by choosing the location the competitor does not know about.

Chimpanzees initially choose randomly in object choice tests like that depicted in Figure 4.2, although they eventually learn to use relevant cues such as whether the person is facing them (Povinelli & Eddy, 1996). However, pet dogs and some other domesticated animals immediately choose a container gestured toward or gazed at by a human. On one interpretation, domestication led to dogs evolving an innate or very early-developing theory of the human mind. More consistent with the fact that selection works through modifying developmental programs is the view

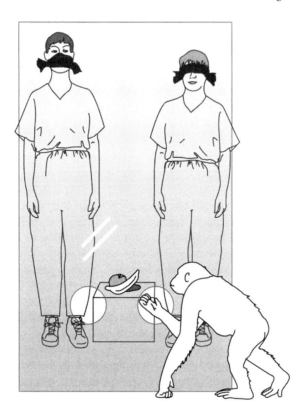

FIGURE **4.2.** Object choice test for chimpanzees. The animal will receive food for gesturing in front of the experimenter who can see him. After photographs in Povinelli and Preuss (1995) with permission.

that as a result of being selected not to fear humans and to attend closely to human behavior, pet dogs learn very early about the significance of human gestures (Reid, 2009; Udell, Dorey, & Wynne, 2010).

The studies with dogs underline the fact that theory of mind tasks like that in Figure 4.2 test responses to cues from helpful humans. A more natural task for chimpanzees is responding to cues from another chimpanzee who is competing for food. Indeed, in such tasks chimpanzees do keep track of what a competitor sees or saw, and hence knows about, by preferentially approaching alternative sources of food (Hare, Call, Agnetta, & Tomasello, 2000). An analogous situation confronts a food-storing bird when a competitor watches it caching, and accordingly ravens and scrub jays discriminate between caches observed by another bird and those not so observed (Emery & Clayton, 2009a). For instance, when recovering caches in private, a scrub jay is more likely to recache items another bird witnessed it caching, a behavior that should help to defeat pilfering. Moreover, when recovering in the presence of another bird, they behave differently toward caches that individual watched them make, apparently encoding "who" along with what, when, and where in their episodic-like memory (Chapter 2; Dally, Emery, & Clayton, 2006). Similarly, when a competitor that witnessed hiding of a given cache is nearby, a raven will move more quickly to retrieve it than if an ignorant competitor is present (Bugnyar & Heinrich, 2005).

The studies just summarized and many others (cf. Byrne & Bates, 2010; Emery & Clayton, 2009a) reveal sophisticated responses to present and/or remembered cues to what other individuals know, intend, or want, but none of them compels us to conclude that the subjects understand knowing, intending, wanting, or the like as mental states. This viewpoint (Penn & Povinelli, 2007; Povinelli & Vonk, 2004) suggests that sophisticated social behavior is supported by *behavioral abstractions*, concept-like representations (Chapter 2) that integrate information about a possible competitor's identity, past and present gaze direction, and the like to control behavior in a flexible and appropriate way.

If behavioral abstractions do the same job as theory of mind without attributing to animals the ability to reason about the unseen mental causes of behavior, is there any way to isolate behavior based specifically on theory of mind? One suggestion (Penn & Povinelli, 2007) involves a complex object choice task with multiple locations designed to distinguish reasoning about theory of mind from both control by observable cues alone and random choice. Another is based on the controversial notion that theory of mind requires generalizing from one's own experiences to those of others. For instance, because I experience seeing when I gaze at something, I infer that others do. This view inspired Heyes (1998) to suggest a paradigm in which animals are first taught that one kind of visor allows them to see things whereas another kind is opaque. If subjects infer others' experiences from their own, then in an object choice task they will treat another individual wearing the see-through visor as knowledgeable and one wearing the opaque visor as ignorant. Reportedly, this test has been tried unsuccessfully with chimpanzees, but young children pass it (see Penn & Povinelli, 2007). Yet another approach is to suggest that full-blown theory of mind has multiple components, with understanding of goals and intentions distinct from understanding of knowledge and beliefs, and that chimpanzees have the former but not the latter (Call & Tomasello, 2008). Chimpanzees and some other primates are indeed sensitive to cues to a person's intention, for instance, responding differently to apparently accidental as opposed to intended acts, but these findings seem explicable in terms of sensitivity to behavioral cues.

This last approach is consistent with a growing appreciation that "Do animals have theory of mind?" is one of those all-or-nothing questions like "Do animals count" that is better answered by asking instead, "What are the components of this ability, which are shared across which species, and why?" Current comparative research seems to be moving in this direction (Emery & Clayton, 2009a). In that, it is converging with new research and theorizing about human theory of mind, which suggests that in adults it has two components: a fast, efficient, early-developing, behavior-reading process and a slower, gradually developing, mind-reading process (Apperly & Butterfill, 2009). The former is used in ongoing social interactions, when we respond rapidly to social signals, whereas the latter comes into play for reasoning about and explaining other people's behavior. The former, but not the latter, is present in very young infants and nonhuman animals. Both are present in adults, as shown by the effects of making them conflict. For example, adult subjects report the number of objects in a display more slowly if the scene includes an avatar whose gaze takes in a different number of objects from the subject's, as if another's viewpoint is processed automatically and unconsciously. Such findings (see Apperly & Butterfill, 2009) indicate that just as nonverbal numerosity discrimination is not replaced by verbal counting during human development (Chapter 3), fast automatic behavior reading is not replaced by mind reading but exists in parallel with it.

Cooperation and Prosocial Behavior

Helping others potentially increases their fitness at a cost to one's own. Because evolutionary theory emphasizes that natural selection occurs primarily at the level of genes promoting the fitness of individuals, altruism is therefore a puzzle. Nevertheless, three kinds of helpful behavior could still evolve by individual selection alone (Trivers, 1971). The study of animal cooperation has generally focused on documenting examples of them rather than analyzing their underlying psychology. However, each kind of altruistic behavior implies particular cognitive and/or emotional mechanisms, most of which are among the basic cognitive tools discussed in Chapter 2.

The least problematic in evolutionary terms is helping relatives. Even if the helper incurs a substantial cost, it may be able to enhance its own fitness by increasing the chances that those who share its genes will reproduce. Thus, altruism could evolve by *kin selection*. A helper does not understand kinship as such but is simply more likely to perform potentially helpful behavior in the presence of individuals possessing some feature shared by its relations. For example, Belding's ground squirrels are more likely to alarm call—thus attracting a predator's attention to themselves—when in the presence of conspecifics raised in the same nest with them, a feature correlated with kinship in natural conditions (Holmes & Mateo, 2007).

A second cognitively undemanding form of cooperation is *mutualism*, an interaction from which both individuals gain an immediate benefit as in "you scratch my back while I scratch yours." Some chimpanzees hunt cooperatively (Boesch & Boesch-Acherman, 2000), and in the lab pairs of apes or monkeys can learn to work together to obtain food from an apparatus that neither could operate by itself (Noë, 2006). Such interactions imply the ability to recognize other individuals and their behaviors and to learn through reinforcement. Mutualistic exchanges need not be with conspecifics. The best-studied example is that of some cleaner fish and their "clients" (Bshary & d'Souza, 2005) on tropical reefs. By eating parasites from larger fish, cleaners get a meal; by making their clients more comfortable, they reinforce clients for visiting. Clients learn to visit particular cleaners at their stations on the reef, using both individual experience and information gained from observing cleaners' behavior toward others. This is a remarkably fine-tuned and complex system, but one based only partly on specifically social cognition.

Reciprocal altruism is arguably a different story. Consistent with evolution by individual selection, reciprocal altruists both benefit from cooperating, but some of the benefits are delayed, as in "You scratch my back now and I'll give you food later." Reciprocity seems to pose cognitive challenges (Cheney, 2011; Stevens & Hauser, 2004): participants must be sensitive to delayed rewards, which are generally not very effective (Chapter 3), and in a social group of any size, they seem to need sophisticated mental balance sheets. Perhaps because of this, there are few if any clear cases of reciprocal altruism between nonrelatives (Clutton-Brock, 2009). Moreover, individuals may interact frequently because they stay close together for some extraneous reason so analysis of relevant field data needs to control for the possible confound of proximity. Models based solely on proximity (Hemelrijk, 2011) serve as a null hypothesis against which to evaluate claims that reciprocation reflects memory for past exchanges. Nevertheless, some recent analyses of data from primates in the field convincingly show animals consistently choosing specific partners to exchange support in aggressive interactions, grooming, and food (Cheney, 2011; Schino & Aureli, 2009). The mechanism that sustains it could be a partner-specific emotional memory, similar to associative strength in summarizing past costly and beneficial interactions in a single value. Episodic memory for the details of past exchanges is not required.

Although the primary force in evolution is individual selection, natural selection can also operate at the level of the group (Wilson & Wilson, 2008). Under conditions arguably resembling those early in hominid evolution, groups of cooperating individuals have an advantage, and this may account for the presence in humans of what is known as *strong reciprocity* or a sense of fairness. In simple economic games, people worldwide exhibit a sense of fairness, tending to divide resources evenly rather than taking all for themselves even when there is no penalty for doing so and wanting to punish others who do not do the same. Such prosocial (or other-regarding) behavior implies a basic ability to perceive what others are getting and compare it to one's own payoffs. Evidence for it in nonhuman primates is mixed (Silk & House, 2012). In one candidate demonstration (Brosnan & de Waal, 2003) capuchin monkeys seeing a neighbor rewarded with a preferred grape when they received only cucumber rejected the cucumber more often than when both got the same reward for their efforts. But several factors other than aversion to social inequity may play a role in tests like this one (Brosnan, Talbot, Ahlgren, Lambeth, & Schapiro, 2010). For example, in itself seeing grapes or memory of past grape rewards may increase rejection of cucumber (Wynne, 2004).

A test free of this confound allows the animal to choose between delivering reward to itself and for the same effort delivering that reward to itself and one to another nearby individual. Because chimpanzees are phylogenetically closer to humans than are other nonhuman primates except for the rarer bonobos (see Fig. 1.2 in Chapter 1), they have been tested the most for this kind of prosocial behavior. However, despite evidence that human children prefer fairness by the age of 3 or 4 years, chimpanzees seem to care only what they themselves are getting (Silk & House, 2012; Warneken & Tomasello, 2009). For example, in the experiment depicted in Figure 4.3, a version of the so-called ultimatum game for testing humans, chimpanzees making the first choice chose the allotment giving them more raisins, and recipients accepted any allotment with at least one raisin for themselves (Jensen, Call, & Tomasello, 2007). However, some monkeys choose to benefit others in tests of prosociality.

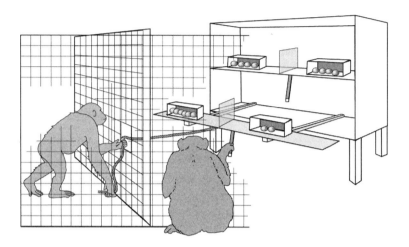

FIGURE **4.3.** Ultimatum game for chimpanzees. The animal on the left (the proposer) has chosen the lower tray, giving him the larger proportion of the eight raisins. The animal on the right (the responder) can complete delivery of this unfair allotment, six raisins to the proposer and two to himself, by pulling the vertical rod, or he can refuse to pull. After Jensen et al. (2007) with permission.

Understanding the species differences in this relatively new area of research is a challenge for the future (Silk & House, 2012). Testing methods may also be crucial. Chimpanzees given a less elaborate test than the one depicted in Figure 4.3 did choose to benefit a partner at somewhat above chance levels (Horner, Carter, Suchak, & de Waal, 2011).

Suggestions that chimpanzees are indifferent to others' welfare have been controversial because they seem inconsistent with observations of spontaneous species-typical helpful behaviors in naturalistic situations, such as a chimpanzee placing an arm over the shoulder of the loser in a fight. These have sometimes been taken as evidence for empathy (de Waal, 2008), that is, an emotional reaction to others' distress that motivates helping. Many animals, including mice and fish, respond physiologically and/ or behaviorally to witnessing conspecifics in pain or acting fearfully or aggressively. As we see in the next section, such empathic responses may support Pavlovian conditioning, but even if they occur in the situations used to test prosociality there may be limits to the arbitrary instrumental responses they can support (de Waal, 2008; Silk & House, 2012).

Social Learning

The Basics

Social learning is any learning from other individuals. It is thus a generic term covering a variety of learning mechanisms, some also used in non-social situations. Similarly, *copying* refers to doing what others are doing, regardless of mechanism. *Imitation*, performing an act because of seeing it done, is perhaps the most cognitively complex form of copying. Learning by imitating was traditionally the holy grail of social learning studies, while other kinds of social learning were dismissed as uninteresting alternatives to be ruled out in attempts to demonstrate imitation. Perhaps as a result, authors do not always agree on terms and definitions for these other processes (Hoppitt & Laland, 2008).

Notwithstanding its importance in human development, imitation is rare in other species, but other kinds of social learning often contribute to mate choice, foraging, enemy recognition, and other behaviors (Kendal, Galef, & van Schaik, 2010; Laland, Atton, & Webster, 2011; Whiten, Hinde, Stringer, & Laland, 2011). Appreciation of this fact together with interest in whether any other species have an analog to human culture has inspired mathematical models dealing with such issues as when and what to learn from others (see Rendell et al., 2011). But although a benefit of sociality is the opportunity to learn from others, behavior would not track environmental change very well if everyone learned socially and no one from individual experience. This insight has stimulated functional models and experimental studies of tradeoffs between socially and individually acquired information. For example, what does an animal do when it learned for itself that A is a more profitable foraging option but others are choosing B (Galef, 2009a; Laland et al., 2011; Rieucau & Giraldeau, 2011)? Findings in this area are generally interpreted functionally, in terms of "social learning strategies," but they raise interesting mechanistic questions. For instance, do they reflect basic mechanisms of attention or memory or rather species-specific predispositions for weighting social versus other cues?

Any test of social learning requires one or more *demonstrators*, animals that perform the behavior of interest, and one or more groups of naive *observers* exposed to the to-be-learned behavior or—as in the example shortly to be discussed—some product of it. Observers are then tested for performance of the target behavior in the absence of demonstrators. Perhaps the most thoroughly analyzed example of mammalian social learning in the laboratory, social transmission of food preferences in rats (Galef, 2007), provides an illustration. Demonstrator rats eat one of two flavored foods, say cinnamon or chocolate, and then interact with observer rats in the absence of food. Observers later given both cinnamon- and chocolate-flavored foods eat a larger proportion of the food eaten by their demonstrator than do observers whose demonstrators ate the alternative. The key to this phenomenon is that when rats meet they engage in face-to-face contact, allowing one to experience the odor of whatever the other has been eating simultaneously with the odor of carbon disulphide, a component of rat breath. The resulting social learning is robust enough that preference can be transmitted across several successive groups or "generations" of observers in the laboratory.

In the wild several additional mechanisms help to insure that naive rats eat foods being safely eaten by others in their colony. For instance, rats approach other rats that are feeding, or even fresh rat droppings. They are thereby exposed to the flavors of safe foods, reducing their neophobia toward them. In social learning terms, the effect of cues from other feeding rats is an example of *local* or *stimulus enhancement*. That is, the activities of other animals increase the attractiveness of a location or stimulus, respectively, which the observer may then learn about on its own. The learning instigated by local or stimulus enhancement often depends on species-specific preferences. Chickens approach other chickens pecking and peck the same colored grain they are pecking at, but they are probably not interested in rat excrement or rat breath.

Cues with species-specific motivational or reinforcing properties also contribute to *observational conditioning*, but here initially neutral cues are associated with a demonstrator's behavior or the motivational state it arouses in observers. One well-studied example involves the mobbing behavior that small birds show toward predators. In mobbing, birds approach a predator in a group, often with special calls and postures. Mobbing alerts others to the presence of the predator and may drive it away. Young blackbirds learn what to mob by seeing what others are mobbing. In a laboratory setup, mobbing by a demonstrator toward a stuffed owl elicits mobbing by an observer who sees only a harmless object such as a milk bottle. The observer starts mobbing the milk bottle, and when later tested alone, it still does so (Curio, 1988). Monkeys acquire fear to objects they see other monkeys reacting fearfully toward (Mineka & Cook, 1988), and they do so more quickly if the object is a snake than a flower, an example of belongingness in associative learning (Chapter 2). There is some evidence that people have a similar adaptive predisposition for fear learning (Öhman & Mineka, 2001).

Imitation

Unlike mobbing or fearful responses to a predator, imitative behaviors are often novel or unusual behaviors for a species, though they need not be. Many candidate examples are behaviors judged difficult to learn by trial and error, as in tool using. One of the original tests of animal imitation learning, Thorndike's study of chicks described in Chapter 1, introduced a design that is key in more recent experimental work: two responses are available (turning left or right in a maze in Thorndike's study); some observers see one demonstrated, some see the other. All are then compared in the absence of demonstrators to see whether observation influences their responses. In one contemporary example of what is now known as *the two-action test*, quail or pigeons that have watched conspecifics operate a treadle for food by either pecking or stepping on it are subsequently more likely to perform the action they saw than are those who saw the alternative. Here both actions are directed toward the same part of the same object, so this two-action test controls for local or stimulus enhancement (see Hoppitt & Laland, 2008).

Because imitation seems so important in human development and because, as will be discussed shortly, chimpanzees exhibit many complex skills in the wild, chimpanzees have been common subjects in studies of imitation learning. Figure 4.4 comes from a direct comparison of children and chimpanzees in a two-action test with an "artificial fruit," a box that could be opened by twisting or poking two bolts. The results are typical in that chimpanzees imitated to some extent but young children were more likely to do so (Whiten, Custance, Gomez, Teixidor, & Bard, 1996). Indeed, children are more likely to engage in blind (or over-) imitation, copying extraneous nonfunctional aspects of a demonstration (see Whiten, McGuigan, Marshall-Pescini, & Hopper, 2009).

Rather than imitating in box-opening or tool-using tasks, chimpanzees sometimes show *emulation* or *affordance learning*. In emulation, the animal appears to learn that there is a goal to be obtained (goal emulation) or that an object has to be used to obtain it. The resulting behavior is not an exact copy of the demonstrator's action but a crude approximation,

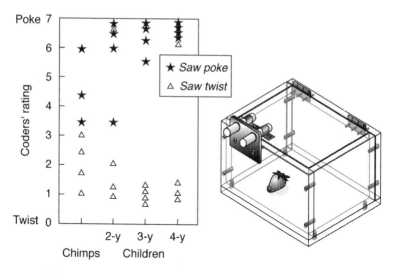

FIGURE **4.4.** Data from chimpanzees and 2-, 3-, and 4-year-old children presented with the "artificial fruit" at right as a function of whether the subjects
had seen a human adult demonstrator poke or twist the cylindrical bolts on its
upper left corner. Each data point represents one subject, rated as to whether
actions on the bolts more resembled poking or twisting. Redrawn from Whiten
et al. (1996) with permission.

such as picking up a rake tool upside down (Tomasello, Davis-Dasilva,
Camak, & Bard, 1987). Affordance learning implies learning how something works (what actions it affords), information that may generate the
same action as a demonstrator's but not because of seeing the demonstrator. The nonsocial character of affordance learning is revealed by "ghost
controls" (Hopper, 2010), in which an apparatus is operated remotely as if
by a ghost. For example, pigeons, chimpanzees, and children that watch a
door slide to the left or to the right to reveal a reward tend to push it in the
direction they saw. Affordance learning may have contributed when New
Caledonian crows that had made an apparatus deliver food by poking
their beak or a stick into a tube spontaneously dropped stones down the
tube (Chapter 3). It deserves deeper analysis in nonverbal creatures: how
does seeing something happen translate into making it happen oneself?

The mechanism of true imitation has been more deeply analyzed.
The basic issue is *the correspondence problem*, that is, what cognitive
mechanism allows me to perform the same action I see you perform?

The correspondence problem is most acute with perceptually opaque actions like facial or whole-body movements, because the observer cannot see how well its own actions match those of the demonstrator. By the same token, probably the most widespread form of imitative learning in nature, song learning by birds (Bolhuis, Okanoya, & Scharff, 2010), is not considered cognitively challenging because young birds can (and do) learn by matching the sounds they hear themselves make to the sounds of adults. Discovery of *mirror neurons* in the monkey premotor cortex at first appeared to solve the correspondence problem (see Iacoboni, 2009; Rizzolatti & Fogassi, 2007). Mirror neurons fire both when the monkey performs a particular action and when it sees another individual perform the same action or hears distinctive sounds such as lip smacking associated with the action. Less direct evidence indicates that humans also have mirror neurons. By representing "my actions" and "others' actions" in a unitary way, mirror neurons provide a mechanism for translating between self and other, but they are not a complete neural mechanism for imitation.

One reason is that monkeys are not very good imitators, although—like people—they do respond positively toward others who imitate them (Paukner, Suomi, Visalberghi, & Ferrari, 2009). Moreover, although normal humans do not overtly imitate everything they see, they have a strong unconscious tendency to imitate, as revealed when automatic imitation conflicts with a required action (Heyes, 2009). For instance, a picture of an open hand beside the instruction to "make a fist" slows closing the hand, whereas a picture of a fist accelerates it. Dogs and budgerigars also show evidence of automatic imitation (Range, Huber, & Heyes, 2011). So why is overt imitation normally inhibited, and if it is, what are mirror neurons and automatic imitation for anyway? A provisional answer (see Iacoboni, 2009; Rizzolatti & Fogassi, 2007) is that mirror neurons play a more general role in social cognition in representing the actions of others and perhaps promoting cooperation with those who mirror one's own actions (Paukner et al., 2009).

Evidence that human newborns copy mouth movements suggests that mirror neurons are innate connections between sensory and motor representations of actions. However, the skilled and generalized imitation characteristic of human adults develops gradually and depends on imitative experience, and in other species the actions copied are generally just a few species-typical behaviors (Catmur, Walsh, & Heyes, 2009). These observations are consistent with the proposal (Heyes, 2010) that mirror neurons develop in social species through learning in which sensory input from performing and/or seeing others perform a given action becomes associated with the motor commands for that action, in a process of *associative sequence learning*. For instance, birds copy pecking actions because having often pecked in the company of pecking conspecifics, as when a flock fed together, they have acquired an association between the sight of pecking and the motor commands for it. Support for this proposal comes from demonstrations that in dogs (Range et al., 2011) and people (see Catmur et al., 2009) training to counterimitate (e.g., to spread the fingers when told to "make a fist" and the reverse) reduces or even reverses automatic imitation of the actions involved. Of course, showing a capacity can be modified in adulthood does not rule out that it developed very early in life, before relevant experience, and indeed there could well be a predisposition to acquire the associations embodied in primate mirror neurons. Nevertheless, associative sequence learning theory has the attraction of showing how an apparently special "higher" cognitive process could be constructed from the bottom up, from basic species-general mechanisms.

Do Nonhuman Animals Teach?

This question shifts the focus from learning by observers to cognition and behavior of demonstrators. Teaching in humans implies theory of mind—the teacher understands what the pupil knows and behaves accordingly. Studies of teaching in other species are guided by a functional definition based strictly on behavior (Caro & Hauser, 1992): for teaching to have occurred, experienced animals must incur a cost, and no immediate gain, by engaging in behavior that allows naive individuals to learn something more quickly or that they would not learn otherwise. "Cost" here is used in the behavioral ecological sense of resources contributing to fitness, such as energy used or time spent foraging. Thus, the rat that has just eaten cinnamon-flavored food is not teaching other rats to eat it because rats normally sniff each other's faces when they meet. Most examples of social transmission in wild animals similarly do not imply any special teaching-like behaviors but rather mechanisms in observers that promote learning from the normal activities of experienced conspecifics (Thornton & Raihani, 2010). The primary exceptions involve carnivorous birds and mammals bringing half-dead prey which their young appear to practice killing (see Caro & Hauser, 1992). Such behavior that increases the cost of foraging in the short run could evolve by conferring long-term benefits via offspring that become independent sooner or are more successful predators.

So far the best-documented example of teaching occurs in wild meerkats (*Suricata suricatta*), small social mammals that live in the Southern

African semidesert digging in the sand for scorpions and other invertebrate prey (Hoppitt et al., 2008; Thornton & McAuliffe, 2006). Groups cooperate to feed their young, who follow foraging adults around emitting begging calls. Initially adults offer pups mostly dead or disabled prey. Over a couple of months they offer more intact prey, but scorpions that can sting are less likely than other prey to be offered intact. Because giving live prey to the young has a cost in time spent monitoring the pups' feeding and recapturing escapees, meerkats fulfill two of the criteria for teaching. *(1)* They engage in special behavior toward naive animals that *(2)* has an immediate net cost. Experiments provide evidence for the third criterion for teaching: facilitating learning by the young. For 3 days researchers gave pups in groups matched for age and litter either four extra live scorpions, four dead ones, or an equivalent amount of hard-boiled egg. In a test at the end, those in the first group were most successful in subduing live scorpions. Adult meerkats are not, however, responding to the pup's skill but rather to their begging signals, which change with pup age. Adults with young pups bring more intact prey after hearing recorded calls of older pups, whereas the calls of younger pups stimulate adults to bring more dead prey.

Contemporary research on animal social learning and—as discussed in the next section—the possibility of animal cultures, has uncovered two other candidates for teaching, each in a different animal group. In birds, pied babblers behave so as to allow their nestlings to associate a special costly "purr" call with feeding, a call that summons the young to food once they leave the nest (Raihani & Ridley, 2008). And in ants (*Temnithorax albipennis*), naive foragers follow experienced "teachers" to food (Franks & Richardson, 2006). Leaders incur a cost, in that they slow down when being followed, but what the "pupils" learn has not been well documented. Nevertheless, these findings with species not closely related to humans together with the fact that teaching is rare or nonexistent in chimpanzees and other wild primates (Thornton & Raihani, 2010) compel the conclusion that teaching in other species is not an evolutionary precursor (i.e., homologous) to human teaching. Animals with certain kinds of life histories may teach one thing, whereas in humans theory of mind and other cognitive or motivational capacities make teaching a domain-general skill (Premack, 2007).

Animal Cultures?

Applied to humans, *culture* refers to group-wide, population-specific customs and beliefs transmitted from one generation to another through teaching, language, and in more subtle ways. Culture is thus a product of social cognitive processes. Nonhuman species also have a variety of socially transmitted behaviors (Kendal et al., 2010; Whiten et al., 2011), but these tend to stay the same from one generation to the next. Human culture stands apart from such traditional behaviors in ratcheting up, with one generation improving on (or at least modifying) what it learned from the one before, resulting in products that become ever more complex (Richerson & Boyd, 2005). This suggests it is underpinned by some cognitive and/or motivational mechanism(s) unique to humans (Tomasello, Carpenter, Call, Behne, & Moll, 2005). The quest to characterize them and understand their evolution—and debates about whether there are such mechanisms—has focused most sharply on population-specific behaviors of chimpanzees in the field and comparisons between chimpanzees and human children in the laboratory, but it is increasingly enriched by studies of traditional behaviors by other primates, cetaceans, birds, and even fish (see Laland & Galef, 2009; Whiten et al., 2011).

Key data here are differences in tool use and other behaviors among seven geographically separated groups of wild chimpanzees (Whiten et al., 1999). Over 30 cases were judged unlikely to reflect ecological differences between sites in prey availability and the like but rather to be "cultural," that is, originated by one or a few individuals and transmitted by social learning. This claim is controversial, in part because on some conceptions even multiple behavioral traditions do not add up to culture (Laland & Galef, 2009). Moreover, ecological causes for population differences may not be obvious. For instance, one candidate cultural behavior is "ant dipping," in which the chimpanzee stimulates ants to crawl up a twig or grass stalk and removes them with the hand or mouth. It turns out, however, that more aggressive species of ants are more safely captured with longer tools and use of the hand (Humle & Matsuzawa, 2002). Thus, population differences in techniques may be at least partly explained by how the local ant species shape individual learning (see Mobius, Boesch, Koops, Matsuzawa, & Humle, 2008).

A further objection to equating population-specific behaviors with culture is that *traditional* implies social transmission, and the required information about development of complex behaviors in natural populations is rarely available (Galef, 2009b). Moreover, on some conceptions culture involves teaching and imitation. As we have seen, there is little evidence for teaching in any nonhuman species, and although field observations such as those of young animals watching intently as adults use tools (observations which are not unique to chimpanzees; Ottoni & de Resende, 2005) support the involvement of some form of social learning, that need not be imitation. Indeed, even when young animals observe tool-using adults, they take time to develop skilled use of tools for extracting prey from shells or crevices, evidently through trial-and-error learning (for an example see Bluff et al., 2010).

The obstacles to studying social transmission in wild primates are circumvented in experiments on social transmission in captive groups (Whiten et al., 2009). The basic type of study employs two groups of animals and an apparatus like that illustrated in Figure 4.4 that affords two actions for extracting a reward. An individual from one group is taught one action, and an individual from the other, the other. Then these demonstrators rejoin their respective groups to test whether others adopt the action of the demonstrator. Ideally a third group is also introduced to the apparatus with no trained demonstrator to see whether they learn to open it spontaneously and if so with which technique. Several different tasks have been transmitted among chimpanzees in this way. Similar results come from studies of transmission chains in which one observer learns from a trained demonstrator and then becomes the demonstrator for the next individual and so on (Whiten et al., 2009). Thus, group differences of the sort documented in the field can be supported by the social learning mechanisms available to chimpanzees, but these need not include imitation. Studies like that illustrated in Figure 4.4 suggest that chimpanzees use imitation, emulation, and/or other processes, depending on the task. In comparisons to young children, their imitative responses may not be particularly rigid or long-lasting, and they are less likely than young children to rigidly copy functionally irrelevant features of a task, such as poking a stick into an empty hole before using it to open a door with food behind it. In contrast, once a copied method has become habitual, chimpanzees are less likely than children to copy a different but more rewarding method (Whiten et al., 2009). Such findings suggest that a variety of species differences contribute to the uniqueness of human culture.

Communication

Research on animal communication ranges from analyzing natural communication systems like the honeybee "dance language" to training captive parrots and chimpanzees to use human words. In the context of this book the most important questions are the following: What cognitive processes are involved in animal communication? Which are shared with human language, and what can the answer to this question reveal about how human language evolved?

In the last part of the twentieth century, much effort was expended attempting to teach forms of human language to apes. The animals' accomplishments were greeted as evidence they could use sign language or systems of tokens comparably to very young children, but in fact they largely learned to use them instrumentally, to get things they wanted. They did not communicate to acquire or share information, nor did they develop grammar in any meaningful sense. Most researchers have now concluded that these studies are most instructive for what the animals did *not* do (for reviews see Fitch, 2010; Shettleworth, 2010a). Just as young song sparrows exposed to swamp sparrow song do not learn to sing it (Marler & Peters, 1989), so apes exposed to the species-typical experiences of human children do not acquire human language. Contemporary research has moved on to examine the degree to which specific components of language are shared with other primate and nonprimate species. Such research receives most attention here. First, however, we review the basics of animal communication.

Animal Communication: Concepts and Controversies

Any instance of communication involves a *signaler* and a *receiver*. A *signal* in this context is "any act or structure that alters the behaviour of other organisms, which evolved because of that effect, and which is effective because the receiver's response has also evolved" (Maynard Smith & Harper, 2003, p. 3). Examples of communicative structures are the warning colors of Monarch butterflies and poison-arrow frogs, i.e. conspicuous colors and patterns signaling distastefulness to predators, evolved because predators readily learn to avoid them (Ruxton, Sherratt, & Speed, 2004). *Cues*, in contrast, are correlated with some feature of an animal but have not evolved specifically because of it. For example, visible symptoms of sickness like a slow gait would not be regarded as signals even though predators may learn to use them to target weak individuals.

Two contrasting views of animal communication are exemplified by the approach of classical ethology on the one hand and the philosophical analysis of human language on the other. As documented by Tinbergen, Lorenz, and other ethologists, social interactions of courting or fighting birds, fish, and other animals are intricate chains of stimulus and response. The stimuli are provided by *displays*, distinctive postures and/ or calls by one member of a pair that elicit specific responses by the other. These in turn might elicit further responses by the first signaler, and so on until mating occurs or a fight is resolved. Everyday examples are the bowing and cooing of a courting male pigeon or the growling and teeth-baring of a hostile dog, an example compared by Darwin (1879/2004) to human emotional expression.

The ethological approach to communication is behavioristic: what is the signal, under what circumstances is it given, and what is the response? Behavioral ecology continues this tradition but focuses on evolution and function. For example, what are the fitness benefits of conspicuous, energy-demanding displays and structures like the tails of peacocks and how can these outweigh their obvious costs? But communication via human language involves intentionality and representations in the minds of signaler and receiver: I have something in mind and I want you to know it (see Dennett, 1983). Communicating thus implies theory of mind: a speaker adjusts his communication to what he believes the audience already knows. This framework has influenced much recent research on animal communication, in some views too much so (Rendall, Owren, & Ryan, 2009; but see Seyfarth et al., 2010). It has, however, led to discoveries that arguably would not have been made otherwise, some involving important differences between animal signaling systems and human language. Current research points toward a synthesis of ethological and cognitivist or informational views, as can be seen in examples from some well-studied animal communication systems.

Honeybee "Dance Language"

When a honeybee returns to the hive from a successful foraging trip, she performs a *waggle dance* on the vertical surface of a honeycomb, while other bees crowd around her (Fig. 4.5). The dance consists of a straight run during which the bee buzzes and waggles her abdomen from side to side, followed by circling back to the start, first to one side then to the other, in a figure 8. The angle of the straight run to vertical matches the angle between the sun's azimuth and the straight-line path to food (see Fig. 4.5), and its duration corresponds to the distance to food. The dance thus carries information about where the forager has just found nectar or another resource, and several kinds of experiments show that bees can use it (Dyer, 2002). In pioneering studies of the dance, Karl von Frisch (1953) found the largest numbers of new recruits at the distance or direction signaled by the dancer. In later experiments the location signaled was not a location recently visited by bees, eliminating the possibility recruits use some environmental cue such as odors of recent visitors. For example, recruits follow the dance of a robot bee or of a live bee induced to "lie" (see Dyer, 2002). Recruited bees caught as they leave the hive and released a few hundred meters away fly the distance and direction

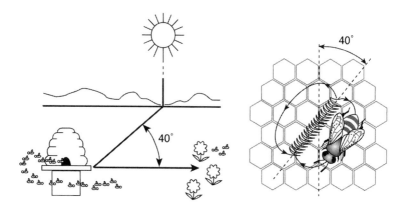

FIGURE **4.5.** The waggle dance of the honeybee showing how its angle to the vertical is related to the angle between the path to the food and the sun's azimuth (the point on the horizon directly below the sun). Redrawn from Seeley (1985) with permission.

indicated by the dance and then start circling around as if searching for the expected nectar source, suggesting they treat the dance as a set of flying instructions rather than information about a location on a cognitive map (Riley, Greggers, Smith, Reynolds, & Menzel, 2005).

The dance language has a history of controversy (Dyer, 2002). Most recently this has revolved around not whether bees *can* use the information in the dance but the extent to which they *do* use it (Grüter & Farina, 2009). Instead of visiting a novel location indicated by the dance, experienced foragers may be stimulated by floral odors on the dancer to visit a familiar site with the same odor, as if having had their memory of it reactivated. Still, as the foregoing summary indicates, the honeybee dance fits the classical ethological description of communication very well.

Audience Effects

Because animals should not evolve to expend energy and attract the attention of predators by signaling unless a receiver is within range, senders should be sensitive to the presence of conspecifics. But such sensitivity does not require theory of mind. Like associatively learned responses (Chapter 2), signaling may be conditional upon contextual cues. For instance, after finding nectar of a given concentration, a returning honeybee forager dances longer when resources are more needed in the hive, as indicated by how fast workers unload her (Seeley, 1995). What would more conventionally be called audience effects are shown by alarm calling roosters (Zuberbühler, 2008). They give more "aerial alarm" calls to a video hawk overhead when a hen is visible than when alone or with a quail as audience, even when the hen "audience" is presented on video so the rooster cannot be influenced by her direct response to the predator (Karakashian, Gyger, & Marler, 1988). Food calling, part of roosters' courtship, also shows audience effects (Evans & Marler, 1994). But such effects do not mean the rooster or any other animal signals with intent to inform. Indeed, consistent with the lack of other evidence for animal theory of mind, there is little evidence from any nonhuman species for sensitivity to receivers' need to know. For example, animals may keep on alarm calling even when receivers have already spotted the predator themselves (Seyfarth & Cheney, 2003; Zuberbühler, 2009).

Functional Reference
The discovery that vervet monkeys have different alarm calls for snakes, eagles, and leopards (Seyfarth, Cheney, & Marler, 1980) suggested that animal vocalizations are like words in referring to things in the world (Radick, 2007). Many other species are now known to have predator-specific alarm calls (Zuberbühler, 2009), but it is hard to know what representation, if any, such calls evoke in receivers (Manser, 2009). Just as in the study of metamemory, planning, and elsewhere, the solution to this problem is to develop clear behavioral criteria, here for *functional reference*. A functionally referential vocalization is, first, given under a restricted set of conditions, that is, it is production specific. Production specificity is demonstrated when the sender is alone, uninfluenced by receivers' responses to whatever caused his signal. For instance, in the laboratory setup described earlier, roosters give different alarm calls to a raccoon at the side of the cage than to the aerial predator. On the receiver's side, functionally referential calls by themselves, in the absence of whatever elicits them, evoke distinctive behaviors. For instance, a caged hen hearing a recorded "aerial alarm" crouches down and looks up, whereas on hearing the "ground predator alarm" she stands tall and looks from side to side (C. S. Evans, Evans, & Marler, 1993).

Responses to a functionally referential alarm call are not necessarily mediated by a representation of the predator, nor need they be entirely learned. A "leopard alarm" might directly elicit running to the nearest tree (the appropriate defense) or it might evoke thoughts of a leopard in the receiver's mind and thereby cause running. Higher orders of representation are conceivable, if unlikely. For instance, the receiver infers that the sender sees a leopard nearby and wants him to run to the trees (Dennett, 1983). The habituation/dishabituation method introduced in Chapter 2 provides a way to address this issue, using acoustically different vocalizations which signal the same event. An excellent example comes from Diana monkeys.

On sighting a leopard or eagle, a male Diana monkey gives a predator-specific call, and nearby females respond with a series of alarm calls of their own. If the male calls again a few minutes later, females show habituation, calling less than the first time, but their calling is renewed if they hear the male alarm associated with a different predator. This dishabituation is due to the change in predator signaled (the "meaning" of the call) rather than to a mere acoustic change, as shown by making use of the fact that females also alarm call in response to the predators' own vocalizations (Zuberbühler, Cheney, & Seyfarth, 1999). Females heard a recorded male eagle alarm, the shriek of an eagle, or male leopard alarms and 6 minutes later, the shriek of an eagle. The first two groups showed equally little alarm calling to this standard probe stimulus. Similarly, the growl of a leopard elicited little alarm calling if the females had recently heard a leopard growl or male leopard alarms. It is as if a common representation of information provided by the calls mediates responding to them, as in category learning or many-to-one matching to sample (Chapter 2).

The aptness of this comparison is confirmed by the observation that species living in close proximity, experiencing similar threats, learn to respond to each other's alarm calls. Some of this learning is quite subtle, as when Diana monkeys respond with silent escape to guinea fowl alarms after hearing people in the area but with leopard alarm calls when they have recently heard leopard growls, as if inferring whether a person or a leopard caused the birds to call (see Zuberbühler, 2009). Here, members of the heterospecific monkey "audience" are eavesdropping on the guinea fowl (Peake, 2005). More generally *eavesdropping* refers to any case in which a third party acquires information from a communicative interaction between other individuals. The information might also be about social relationships (Cheney & Seyfarth, 2005a; Seyfarth & Cheney, 2010), as when animals learn about others' dominance relationships by watching them interact (Chapter 3).

Urgency and Emotion

Predator-specific alarm calls should evolve when the environment affords different evasive responses for different predators, as in climbing higher to avoid leopards versus descending from the tree canopy to avoid eagles (Donaldson, Lachmann, & Bergstrom, 2007). But when the habitat affords only one means of escape, the only important information about an approaching predator is how near and/or dangerous it is, and this can be communicated by a single type of alarm call varying in intensity (e.g., loudness or repetition rate). For instance, open grassland species such as Belding's ground squirrels have one alarm call whose intensity reflects the urgency of need to break off other activities and run to the burrow (see Furrer & Manser, 2009). Similarly, black-capped chickadees' alarm calls have more "dee" notes for more dangerous predators (Templeton, Greene, & Davis, 2005). Urgency-based alarm calling fits a traditional notion that signals are expressions of emotion (here, fear) that directly elicit receivers' responses (Rendall et al., 2009). But referential alarm calling can also reflect urgency. For instance, like vervet monkeys, meerkats have acoustically distinct alarm calls for snakes, other ground predators, and aerial predators, but each call type varies in intensity with the strength of threat posed by the given predator. Call intensity determines the completeness and duration of receivers' responses (see Furrer & Manser, 2009).

Animal Communication and Human Language

Attempts to teach human language to apes (see Fitch, 2010; Shettleworth, 2010a) essentially asked, "Can another animal learn language?" In the early twenty-first century, this all-or-nothing question has been replaced by asking which components of language, or communicative ability, are shared with other species, to what degree, and why. For example, animal signals contain information, in that particular signals are correlated with particular states of the world (Seyfarth et al., 2010), and receivers use this information, but signalers do not seem to signal with the intent to inform. Another difference from human language is that although we can communicate an infinity of messages, even the graded signals of alarm-calling ground squirrels or dancing honeybees communicate about only a few things. Not only does any human language have many more words than any known nonhuman communication system has signals, words are combined according to implicit grammatical rules to make new messages, whereas in only a few known cases do nonhuman species combine discrete signals in predictable ways. Moreover, it still is unclear whether sequences of two different alarm calls or the like necessarily have "meaning" systematically related to their components (see Zuberbühler, 2009).

This sort of broad comparative approach to language was prominently articulated by Hauser, Chomsky, and Fitch (2002), who proposed that the human language "faculty" in the broad sense includes sensory-motor, conceptual-intentional, and computational components, many of which are shared with other species and not specific to language. The abstract computational capacity by means of which an infinity of meaningful sentences is generated from a finite set of words is referred to by Hauser, Chomsky, and Fitch (2002) as the faculty of language in the narrow sense. Crucially, it includes the ability to comprehend and generate recursive structures, an ability Hauser et al. suggest is unique to humans. Recursion refers to the embedding of a unit inside another unit of the same kind, as in "The rabbit the fox saw ran." Formally, interpreting any such sentence with an AABB structure (where any number of *A*s are subjects and the same number of *B*s are predicates) requires a *phrase structure grammar*, an implicit understanding that respective *A*s are matched with respective *B*s. Cognitively less demanding is stringing elements together, or *finite state grammar*, ABAB..., as in "The fox saw the rabbit that ran."

Although the proposal that recursion is the key unique feature of the human language faculty is controversial (Fitch, 2005; Pinker & Jackendoff, 2005), phrase structure grammar is generally agreed to be a key characteristic of human language. This view has inspired tests of whether animals can discriminate strings of sounds with a simple recursive structure such as AABB from equal length strings of the same sounds obeying a finite state grammar (e.g., ABAB). In the most thorough study to date (van Heijningen, deVisser, Zuidema, & ten Cate, 2009) zebra finches learned to discriminate five strings of one type from five of the other, where the stimuli were "artificial songs" constructed of elements from natural zebra finch song. The birds transferred, with some decrement, to new exemplars constructed with the same song units. However, tests with sequences of two new song units (i.e., C and D) showed that they were not in fact responding to the overall structures but to local features such as whether the stimulus ended in two *B*s.

As evidenced by the attention given this and similar studies (see, e.g., Corballis, 2007), shifting the focus from a global ability such as language (or numerical cognition, planning, etc.) to its components does not bring an end to all-or-nothing debates. Here, the question has shifted from "Do any animals have language?" to "Do any have recursion?" but researchers still confront the potentially endless task of finding a species that passes an unassailable test. In any case, not all agree that recursion alone makes human language unique. Rather, language may be a unique combination of components, coevolved under special conditions in early hominid society (Pinker & Jackendoff, 2005). Just as assumed by the tests of recursion, some concepts expressed in or implicit in language may be present in other cognitive domains even if not expressed in communication. For instance, Cheney and Seyfarth (2005b) suggest that studies of baboon social cognition (e.g., Bergman et al., 2003) reveal implicit understanding of hierarchical classification. They also suggest that baboons' responses to sequences of vocalizations representing social interactions imply understanding of simple narrative structure like "A is approaching B and B is rebuffing her." Other candidates include aspects of spatial and numerical cognition and sensitivity to sequential organization (Hauser et al., 2002). The last of these has been shown very well by dolphins trained to respond to a complex system of commands. For example, in one of the few demonstrations of animal sensitivity to syntax, they discriminated between sequences such as "take the ball to the hoop" and "take the hoop to the ball" (Herman & Uyeyama, 1999; Kako, 1999).

The fact that apes extensively exposed to forms of human language learn to produce it in only a very limited way indicates that learning language requires some specialized process(es) unique to humans. Candidates include theory of mind together with a motivation to share information that communicating chimpanzees rarely if ever seem to display (Tomasello et al., 2005). As for possibly specialized learning processes per se, what allows young children to increase vocabulary at seemingly astronomical rates is *fast mapping*. Encountering a novel word together with a novel object or event, the child implicitly understands that the word refers to the object or event and thereby learns its meaning (see Pilley & Reid, 2010). Fast mapping goes beyond learning by exclusion, a capacity shared by sea lions among others (Kastak & Schusterman, 2002), to an understanding of reference, as demonstrated by immediate use of the word in multiple contexts. For instance, having learned "wug," when asked, "bring me the wug," the one new toy among three, a child could later "put the wug beside the teddy." It turns out that this ability is shared with at least one other mammal, a border collie named Chaser (Pilley & Reid, 2010), suggesting that it emerges in some way from extensive experience learning word-object associations. Over 3 years, Chaser learned the names of more than 1,000 objects as well as verbs for several actions he could perform. With the experimenter in a separate room to eliminate Clever Hans effects, he could correctly choose any familiar object from a bigger collection. Like a previously studied border collie, Chaser showed evidence of fast mapping, though like children he did not retain the new associations well without practice. More important, he also correctly pawed, nosed, or took newly named objects the first time he was commanded to do so, thus exhibiting behavior consistent with understanding of reference.

We have so far dealt only with receptive aspects of language, but of course learning to produce language depends on vocal imitation, at least for hearing humans. Evidently crucial elements of the vocal mechanisms and cognitive capacity required for acquiring spoken language were absent in the last common ancestor of chimpanzees and humans and have evolved more recently (Fitch, 2005). Indeed, evidence that learning to produce words vocally, whether by imitation or otherwise, was beyond the abilities of chimpanzees inspired the studies in which apes were taught gestural and other nonvocal systems of communication. But some birds share our ability to acquire an extensive vocal repertoire by imitation, and it turns out that birdsong learning has many instructive similarities to human language learning (see Bolhuis et al., 2010). As already mentioned, both are compelling examples of interactions between experience and species-typical predispositions for learning. Like human babies, songbirds imitate species-typical vocalizations which they hear early in life, at first crudely in a period of subsong analogous to babbling. The brain circuits involved in song learning and production are well understood and have some instructive parallels to those involved in language. In evolutionary terms, the many similarities between birdsong and speech development are not homologies between birds and humans but analogies (i.e., not descended from a common ancestor but convergently evolved), likely reflecting basic constraints on the control and development of complex vocal signals.

The topic of communication thus brings us back to where we began in Chapter 1, with Darwin's claim that human "mental powers" differ in degree and not in kind from those of other animals. In this chapter we seem to have uncovered one "difference in kind," namely the presence in humans of the ability to acquire and use language, a "mental power" that Darwin also pondered (see Seyfarth & Cheney, 2010). Full-blown theory of mind seems to be another candidate, along with a motivation to cooperate in certain ways. Contemporary discussions of Darwin's claim are a major subject of Chapter 5.

Suggestions for Further Reading

Cheney, D. L. (2011). Cooperation and cognition. In R. Menzel & J. Fischer
    (Eds.), *Animal Thinking: Contemporary Issues in Comparative Cognition*.
    (pp. 239–252). Cambridge, MA: MIT Press.
Dyer, F. C. (2002). The biology of the dance language. *Annual Review of
    Entomology*, *47*, 917–949.
Emery, N. J., & Clayton, N. S. (2009). Comparative social cognition. *Annual
    Review of Psychology*, *60*, 17.11–17.27.
Fitch, W. T. (2005). The evolution of language: A comparative review. *Biology
    and Philosophy*, *20*, 193–230.
Heyes, C. (2009). Evolution, development, and intentional control of imitation.
    Philosophical Transactions of the Royal Society B, *364*, 2293–2298.
Hoppitt, W., & Laland, K. (2008). Social processes influencing learning in
    animals. *Advances in the Study of Behavior*, *38*, 105–165.
Hoppitt, W. J. E., Brown, G. R., Kendal, R., Rendell, L., Thornton, A., Webster,
    M. M., et al. (2008). Lessons from animal teaching. *Trends in Ecology and
    Evolution*, *23*, 486–493.
Seyfarth, R. M., & Cheney, D. L. (2010). Production, use, and comprehension in
    animal vocalizations. *Brain & Language*, *115*, 92–100.
Shettleworth, S. J. (2010). Chapters 12–14 in *Cognition, Evolution, and Behavior*
    (2nd ed.). New York: Oxford University Press.
Silk, J. B., & House, B. R. (2012). The phylogeny and ontogeny of prosocial
    behavior. In J. Vonk & Shackelford (Eds.), *Oxford Handbook of
    Comparative Evolutionary Psychology* (pp. 381–398). New York: Oxford
    University Press.
Whiten, A., Hinde, R. A., Stringer, C. B., & Laland, K. N. (2011). Culture
    evolves. *Philosophical Transactions of the Royal Society (London) B*, *366*,
    938–948.

CHAPTER 5
....

Comparative Cognition and Human Uniqueness

esearch discussed in this book has expanded the boundaries of
what we know animals are capable of cognitively. We have seen
evidence for sophisticated feats of memory, numerical and spatial cognition, subtle social intelligence, and flexible tool use, among
other things. It seems there has never before been so much support for
Darwin's (1871, p. 105) conclusion "that the difference in mind between
man and the higher animals, great as it is, is certainly one of degree and
not of kind." But looked at more closely, recent research provides just
as many grounds for questioning Darwin's conclusion as for endorsing
it. Some claims for humanlike capacities in other species are controversial or preliminary, the extent to which functionally similar behaviors
involve similar mechanisms in other animals as in humans frequently
remains to be determined, and behaviors such as tool use or teaching
by species distantly related to humans are shown only in very limited
circumstances. Indeed, recent findings point to some quite specific ways
in which humans are cognitively unique. In this chapter we look at contemporary attempts to characterize human cognitive uniqueness in the
light of material from throughout this book.

Different in Degree or Kind?

When Darwin asserted that human "mental powers" differ "in degree
but not in kind" from those of other species, he meant that other animals share all the cognitive abilities shown by humans, developed to
a lesser degree. Thus, in a chapter that could still serve as a survey of

112

the major topics in comparative cognition, he describes monkeys, dogs, and parrots associating definite sounds with definite meanings as evidence that animals have a small degree of that same ability that is expressed to an "almost infinitely larger" degree in human language (Darwin, 1879/2004, p. 108). Nowadays, as discussed in Chapter 4, the human language faculty is seen as consisting of much more than the ability to associate words with meanings, and indeed the ability to create and understand the recursive structures of human languages may not be shared with any other species. But even if we decide that—in the words of some authors (Penn et al., 2008)—Darwin was mistaken, and humans are cognitively unique in some respect(s), this does not mean we did not evolve by small degrees from the last ancestor we share with chimpanzees and bonobos. Nature provides many examples of apparent "differences in kind" traceable to the accumulation of tiny "differences in degree," as in the evolution of birds from primitive reptiles and snakes from animals with legs. In the case of human cognitive evolution, it is important to remember that although chimpanzees and bonobos are our closest *living* relatives (see Fig. 1.2 in Chapter 1), the last ancestor we share with them is not any species still extant. The still-mysterious path from that unknown ancestor to modern *Homo sapiens* is littered with species that are now extinct, some probably yet to be discovered. And apes have been following their own evolutionary trajectories for the last 5 million years or so. Nevertheless, comparisons of (mostly) chimpanzees and human children provide some of the best evidence available on which to base theories of human uniqueness.

Shared Intentionality

One prominent such theory comes from a research team that has extensively studied all four great ape species (chimpanzees, bonobos, gorillas, and orangutans), often directly comparing them with human children in the same experiments. They (Tomasello et al., 2005) propose that the psychological key to human uniqueness is motivational as much as cognitive, namely a capacity for what they call *shared intentionality*. Well before the age of 1 year, young children participate with others in interactions in which they jointly attend to and act on things in the world. This motivation and ability to share intentions and goals is evident in the early stages of language learning, when children and adults use vocalizations and gestures to communicate about interesting things in the world for the sheer pleasure of it, something even language-trained apes rarely if ever do. Eventually such "cooperative communicative" interactions are informed by full-blown theory of mind, but they are evident long before. They are key to learning the ingredients of culture from adults, where children slavishly imitate details of demonstrations which chimpanzees do not (Chapter 4). Thus, in the view of Tomasello and colleagues (2005), the social cognitive capacity for shared intentionality "scaffolds up" cognitive skills in the physical domain, as in mathematics, map reading, or tool use. Most important, perhaps, the ability to share goals and intentions underlies unique forms of human cooperation.

As the foregoing summary indicates, this proposal can be seen to embrace most of the ape-human differences in social cognitive abilities reviewed in Chapter 4. The assumption that the fundamental ape-human cognitive differences are entirely in the social domain is consistent with results of a comparative study in which 106 chimpanzees, 32 orangutans, and 105 2.5-year-old children were each given a battery of tests of physical and social cognition (Herrmann, Call, Hernández-Lloreda, Hare, & Tomasello, 2007). Children performed similarly to apes on the physical tasks (tests of spatial and numerical cognition and simple tool use) but outperformed the apes on social tasks, especially tests of social learning. Moreover, factor analysis indicated that their intelligence was structured differently, with a separate distinctly social factor needed to account for the performance of children but not chimpanzees (Herrmann, Hernandez-Lloreda, Call, Hare, & Tomasello, 2010). In neither species was there evidence for an overall general intelligence factor (g), underlining the implication that the species difference, at least in this set of tests, is in one particular module or aspect of intelligence. Any proposal for a uniquely human trait should at least suggest how it might have functioned in hypothesized early human social groups, and shared intentionality is on relatively firm ground here, as it is consistent with current ideas about the importance of cooperation in human evolution (Wilson & Wilson, 2008).

The amount of data reported by Herrmann and colleagues (2007) is impressive for comparative behavioral research, but the study is not without its critics. As in any species comparison, it should be asked, were the subjects typical of their species and were the tests equally fair to all (Boesch, 2007)? The children were middle-class Westerners, tested by a member of their own species, in their mothers' presence. Because they were only 2.5 years old, the children had not had much formal instruction, but they may have been more familiar with the general testing format than the apes. The apes were semi-free-ranging captives in primate sanctuaries in their native countries, but of course they were tested by humans, not other apes. Unfortunately, when comparing species that are uncommon in captivity (and in this case, also in the wild), it can be impossible to equate all subjects for developmental history or experience in similar experiments. Nonhuman subjects get their "instructions" largely from trial-and-error learning, whereas people can just be told what to do. Requiring human subjects to learn the rules for themselves can make their performance more like that of other animals (Brosnan et al., 2011; Gibson, 2001). Perfect methodological rigor may not always be attainable in comparative studies with nonhuman primates, but thoroughness should be, in the form of awareness of potential confounds, use of multiple tests (as here), ideally with multiple labs and subject populations, and other practices designed to increase the chances that observed species differences and similarities reflect the factors they are claimed to.

Relational Redescription

On the basis of their extensive studies of theory of mind and physical understanding in captive chimpanzees, Povinelli and colleagues have long claimed that, despite appearances to the contrary, chimpanzees do not understand the world in terms of unobservable mental or physical processes (e.g., Povinelli, 2000; Vonk & Povinelli, 2006). Chimpanzees—and by implication other nonhuman animals—respond to and learn about the perceptible features of events with great sophistication and subtlety, but without implicitly interpreting them in terms of such abstractions as physical forces or other individuals' knowledge and beliefs. As we have seen in Chapters 3 and 4, these controversial claims have played a key role in challenging proponents of more anthropomorphic interpretations to seek less equivocal evidence for humanlike understandings. As we have also seen, some contemporary theorists suggest that many human competences, including theory of mind (Apperly & Butterfill, 2009) and tool use (Osiurak et al., 2010), consist of processes shared with other species together with components unique to humans similar to those described by Povinelli (2000). For example, human social responses are based to some extent on fast efficient "behavior reading" as done by apes and scrub jays, but they can also involve the slower more explicit "mind reading" that children develop during their first 4 or 5 years (Apperly & Butterfill, 2009).

Povinelli and colleagues' proposals (e.g., Povinelli, 2000; Vonk & Povinelli, 2006) are precursors to a more sweeping proposal by Penn,

Holyoak, and Povinelli (2008): the fundamental discontinuity between human and nonhuman minds is in a domain-general ability to represent the perceived features of the world in terms of abstract concepts and relationships. Animals learn rules and respond to categories of perceptible events, behaviors, and things in the world in terms of representations like the "behavioral abstractions" discussed in Chapter 4, but they do not form or reason about higher level representations. This uniquely human ability is dubbed *representational redescription* because it involves redescribing representations of the world in terms of perceptible, first-order features in higher order, abstract terms. For example, in Chapter 2 we saw that although monkeys and pigeons can learn to discriminate visual displays with elements all the same versus different on the basis of perceptual variability, unlike humans they do not acquire an abstract domain-general categorical concept of sameness versus difference (Wasserman & Young, 2010).

Penn et al.'s claim that human cognitive architecture uniquely affords representational redescription at first glance appears incommensurable with Tomasello et al.'s claim that human cognitive uniqueness springs from shared intentionality. But they are different kinds of explanations. Penn et al.'s theory characterizes human-ape discontinuity as observed in adults. It does not address the possibility that special social-emotional-cognitive traits present very early in life drive development of the enormous differences between adults of the two species. The motivational and cognitive processes described by "shared intentionality" may provide at least part of the mechanism by which the unique forms of representation and reasoning characterized by Penn et al. (2008) develop in individual humans growing up in a human culture. Undoubtedly some fundamental species difference in cognitive potential also plays a role, as testified by the repeated failures of apes raised like children to match their human counterparts in language.

Language, Recursion, and Domain Generality

The two theories just sketched are hardly the only ideas about what characterizes human cognitive uniqueness. Traditionally, possession of language has been seen as the primary difference between humans and apes. The results of twentieth-century attempts to teach chimpanzees forms of human language only reinforce this perception. But a classic chicken-and-egg problem stands in the way of explaining all unique human conceptual accomplishments as resulting from the possession of language: the concepts expressed in language would be meaningless to a creature that does not already have them or something like them. This insight suggests that we should be looking for precursors to human linguistic and conceptual abilities in nonverbal concepts implicit in the natural behavior of other species (Hauser et al., 2002). For example, life in a primate social group with ranked families of ranked individuals seems to demand an ability to process hierarchical relationships (Cheney & Seyfarth, 2005b). Such considerations suggest that human language and conceptual ability must have coevolved, with primitive forms of communication providing the capacity to express new or half-formed concepts, leading to more elaborate language, and so on (see Penn et al., 2008).

Of course, coevolution of language and cognition "by degrees" may still have resulted in some human abilities "different in kind" from those of any other contemporary species. One candidate mentioned in Chapter 4 is the ability to generate and understand recursive structures claimed by Hauser, Chomsky, and Fitch (2002) to be the only component of language not shared with other species, their "faculty of language in the narrow sense." A broader related claim (Corballis, 2011) is that although recursion is unique to humans, it is not restricted to—or even always seen in—language. Rather, recursive thinking is the key to human uniqueness. Recursion is construed here very generally as any even implicit inclusion of one kind of thought or knowledge within another, as in using memories to make plans or using understanding of one's own mental states to understand another's.

Finally, Premack (2007) has responded to the recent wave of evidence for unexpectedly humanlike behavior in other species with the observation that examples of animal episodic-like memory, planning, teaching, and so on are all specialized adaptations confined to single domains. For instance, so far as is known meerkats teach their young only food-handling skills and by a mechanism only partly like human teaching (Chapter 4), but people can teach each other almost anything the mind can conceive of. Thus, whereas animals' abilities are domain specific, humans' abilities are domain general, capable of serving many goals, representing an interweaving (Premack, 2010) of domain-specific abilities seen in other species. This is thus another attempt at a unitary characterization of human adult cognitive uniqueness. None is likely to be the whole story since the multitudinous differences between human and animal minds cannot necessarily be boiled down to a single genetic, neural, or conceptual mechanism.

Clues from Modularity and Development

What Is Modularity?

Modularity was defined informally in Chapter 1 as "the property of being made up of somewhat self-contained and independently functioning parts." Complex systems of all sorts seem to demand a hierarchical modular structure so that a part can break down or be modified without the whole ceasing to function (Simon, 1962). Modularity is therefore an essential property of biological systems, from genomes to bodies (West-Eberhard, 2003). Evolvability as we know it may be possible only in modular systems, in which parts of the organism can change while other, well-adapted parts remain relatively unchanged. For instance, new species can result from differences in genes for number of legs or body segments (Carroll, 2005), and the famous Darwin's finch species differ most conspicuously in beak size and shape, which turn out to reflect activity of a common avian gene involved in beak growth (P. R. Grant & Grant, 2008). Similarly, species that encounter extraordinary demands for spatial memory in retrieving stored food or defending large territories may evolve exceptional spatial memories and hippocampi while remaining otherwise cognitively and behaviorally similar to their close relatives (Chapter 1).

But although modularity is an accepted notion in evolutionary and developmental biology, it is deeply controversial in the cognitive sciences. This includes comparative cognition and examples such as the adaptive specializations of memory just alluded to (e.g., Bolhuis & Macphail, 2001). *Modularity* in cognition retains the connotations given it by Fodor (1983) in his seminal discussion, *The Modularity of Mind*, even though Fodor himself did not necessarily require cognitive modules to have all the properties he discussed (see Barrett & Kurzban, 2006). Fodorian modules are domain-specific, peripheral, perceptual (as opposed to central decision-making) mechanisms, innate, fast-acting (like a reflex), unconscious, obligatory (i.e., acting regardless of circumstances), and *encapsulated* (i.e., impervious to information outside their particular domain, as olfaction is impervious to auditory information).

The paradigmatic Fodorian modular process is a visual illusion, encapsulated because even knowing one is seeing an illusion does not prevent it. It is this property that inspired Cheng (1986) to attribute disoriented rats' reliance on the shape of an enclosure and disregard of more informative colored walls and landmarks to a geometric module

(Chapter 3). Young children show the same domination by geometry. With training, disoriented rats learn to use landmarks as well as geometry, and, similarly, children overcome the domination of geometry with age and mastery of spatial language. These findings suggest to some (e.g., Newcombe, Ratliff, Shallcross, & Twyman, 2009) that rather than being modular, processing of spatial geometry is "adaptively combined" with other information from landmarks and the like. Such an either/or approach contrasts with the view discussed later in this section on which the essence of modularity is the specificity of processing rules to content (i.e., information domain; Barrett & Kurzban, 2006). Some degree of modularity is not incompatible with use of multiple information sources.

Some contemporary debates about cognitive modularity focus on the claim by evolutionary psychologists that not only perception but central decision making is "massively modular." The mind is like a Swiss Army knife, entirely made up of separately functioning parts (Cosmides & Tooby, 1994). Some controversial evidence for central modularity comes from demonstrations that how people reason is influenced as much by the content of logical problems as by their abstract formal structure. In the best-studied example, social content, namely detecting cheaters on a social contract, more frequently elicits correct conclusions than do other kinds of content or the abstract *P*s and *Q*s used in traditional tests of logical thinking (Cosmides, 1989; but see J. S. B. T. Evans, 2002). Such findings suggest that reasoning evolved not as a general-purpose device but as an adaptation to specific situations in early hominid society. Similarly, in economic decision making, relative valuation and preference for immediacy (Chapter 3 and Santos & Hughes, 2009) may not maximize payoffs in modern life but were "ecologically rational" (Todd & Gigerenzer, 2007) in our past environments and those of other species. Evolutionary psychology is easy to criticize as postulating a module for everything (cf. Buller, 2005). Indeed, it is not necessarily obvious how to decide what the modules or relevant domains of information are. For instance, space is usually considered an information domain, but we have seen that navigation involves several dissociable, informationally distinct, processes such as path integration, use of landmarks, and so on. Neurobiological analysis reveals yet other processes (Jeffery, 2010). *Domain* thus seems to be a fractal concept.

As so often happens when issues are framed as opposing extremes, the truth is probably somewhere in between (Barrett & Kurzban, 2006). Cognition is to some extent functionally modular, consisting of distinct processes operating on distinct domains of information, but whether any such functional modules are localized in the brain or have the other Fodorian properties is an empirical question (Coltheart, 1999). The comparative research discussed in Chapters 3 and 4 of this book throws functional modularity into sharp relief. Consider the distinct kinds of inputs and different operations on them demanded by spatial, temporal, and numerical cognition, recognition of animacy or social relationships, and so on. Even associative learning, although it is a powerful mechanism for tracking temporal predictiveness and physical causal relationships, is not the general process it was once claimed to be (Gallistel, 1999). But at the same time, the output of different modules must ultimately be integrated in some way to determine action. Outputs are integrated in memory, too, as in episodic-like memory for the what, where, and when of events. A strictly modular view seems to preclude processes like associative learning, attention, or working memory that cut across domains, although it does not preclude separate modules having some properties in common. And what about well-established ideas like general intelligence, for which there is increasing evidence in nonhuman species (Matzel & Kolata, 2010; Reader, Hager, & Laland, 2011)?

Cognitive Modularity, Core Knowledge, and Human Uniqueness

One theme of the preceding chapters is that most of the cognitive processes evident in nonhuman species are shared with humans. A subset of them, referred to as *core knowledge systems*, is the focus of an approach to human cognitive development championed by Carey (2011), Gelman (2009), and Spelke (2000). What counts as a core system varies, but they generally include the precise small number and approximate large number systems, and processing spatial geometry and animacy (in this context, *agency*). Because these fundamental core systems have the same properties in humans as in other species, they appear evolutionarily ancient. Because they are present as early in life as they can be detected, they are referred to—controversially for child development (see, e.g., Newcombe, 2002)—as innate knowledge systems. Importantly, in addition to the core systems (in effect, cognitive modules) that acquire and operate on domain-specific information in characteristic ways, infants have basic mechanisms for learning and conceptual change that cut across core systems (see Gelman, 2009).

In the context of this book, the core knowledge approach is important for the way in which it addresses two key questions about human cognitive uniqueness. First, if the infant starts out with the same core knowledge systems as other species (of primates at least), where does specifically human understanding come from? Saying that it comes from culture is not helpful because this does not explain how anyone acquired such understanding in the first place. There must be some unique developmental mechanism(s) supporting uniquely human forms of understanding. Second, what happens to the innate core mechanisms during development? Are they still present and active in adults or are they transformed into and/or replaced by uniquely human thought? The answers to these questions provided by the core knowledge approach (especially as developed by Carey, 2009, 2011) are important to the story of human cognitive uniqueness.

Numerical cognition is a well-developed case study here. Research reviewed in Chapter 3 shows that human infants and other primates (at least) have two core systems of numerical cognition. The small number or object tracking system precisely encodes numbers up to three or four. All numerosities within this signature range are discriminated equally well. For instance, a baby is as likely to choose three crackers over two crackers as over one. The approximate large number system, in contrast, discriminates sets of any numerosity from one another in a way described by Weber's Law: ratios matter, not absolute differences. But sometime during childhood, children in a numerate culture learn about integers, the counting numbers that precisely label any numerosity, suggesting that the appreciation of number characteristic of the small number system is somehow extended to all numbers. Appreciation of integers as quantities each of which is one more than the one before, on to infinity, is not simply a consequence of learning the sequence of count words "one, two, three ....." It develops gradually, initially perhaps only one integer at a time (see Carey, 2009). A cognitive leap is required for children to realize (if only implicitly) that when any set has one more added to it, the numerosity is always the next number in the count list. Indeed, chimpanzees trained to associate the number symbols with sets of items never seem to grasp this: each new association of symbol with set size takes as long to learn as the one before (Matsuzawa, 2009).

Carey (2009, 2011) explains such conceptual transitions in terms of "Quininan bootstrapping," after the philosopher Quine's discussion of the analogous process in scientific discovery. "Bootstrapping" refers to the fact that the child has to somehow "pull herself up by her own bootstraps," using the concepts and core knowledge she already has to grasp a concept she doesn't yet have. A crucial stage is that at which the child has memorized the count list but still lacks a full concept of integer. Language and culture, likely via the "cooperative communicative interactions" emphasized by Tomasello and colleagues (2005), make essential contributions here because the discrepancy between what the child understands and what she and others around her express is what instigates "bootstrapping" or conceptual change. But even though a person may eventually understand higher mathematics, the original core systems remain intact, as shown by demonstrations that, for instance, the approximate number system can be brought into play with nonverbal tests or in people without number language (Chapter 3).

Parallel Systems, Shared and Unique

The coexistence of a developmentally prior, cognitively simpler, phylogenetically older cognitive system and a later-developing, more complex, uniquely human system characterizes domains other than numerical cognition. In theory of mind, adult humans seem to have both the fast "behavior reading" available to chimpanzees, scrub jays, and other animals, and slowly developing, more explicit, "mind reading" (Apperly & Butterfill, 2009). In addition to biases shared with chimpanzees (Silva et al., 2008), human tool use is supported by both technical knowledge, in effect skills learned instrumentally via species-general mechanisms, and physical causal understanding that other species lack (Osiurak et al., 2010). Same-different discrimination is subserved by a species-general ability to learn discriminations based on perceptual variability and by the uniquely human cross-modal categorical concept (Wasserman & Young, 2010). Similarly, although we share with other species many specific mechanisms for spatial orientation and localization, we also learn to use maps and spatial language (Landau & Lakusta, 2009). And in economic decision making, although we can calculate the actions that maximize payoffs objectively, we still show evolutionarily ancient "irrational" influences of immediacy and relative value (Santos & Hughes, 2009).

This view of human cognitive architecture and its relationship to that of other species suggests that we should be asking how the species-general and the uniquely human systems in different domains interact. Individual (as opposed to social) economic decisions seem to provide examples of conflict, in that evolutionarily ancient biases dictate a suboptimal choice. Shared and unique mechanisms may support each other, or at least not conflict. Often the simple shared mechanism may have a more important role than that acknowledged in a folk psychology that attributes action to conscious reasoning and decision making. Such seems to be the case with theory of mind, where many of our moment-to-moment social interactions result from "fast behavior reading." And how many tool users reason out how a screwdriver works each time they pick one up? Since Darwin, comparative research has emphasized the humanlike accomplishments of other animals, but contemporary research elsewhere in psychology has been revealing ways in which our behavior is often controlled in simpler, more "animal-like" ways than folk psychology suggests (Shettleworth, 2010b).

Conclusions

Any account of human cognitive uniqueness needs to characterize both adult cognition and how it can develop from a starting point so much like that of other species. The successful communication between comparative and developmental psychologists illustrated by research on numerical cognition, spatial behavior, theory of mind, and tool use will be key in contributing to a balanced understanding of the interplay among mechanisms common to many species and the uniquely human aspects of cognition. The account based on the core knowledge approach has much to offer, but it is unlikely to explain everything. For instance, humans are capable of symbolic thought, whereas other animals are generally believed not to be (see Penn et al., 2008). Of the human abilities examined in this book, those involving mental time travel seem to elude other species, so far at least. The resulting inability to plan shows itself, among other ways, in animals' limited ability to combine multiple tools for solving new tasks. Another possibly uniquely human ability, related to time travel in that we experience it in conscious thought, is genuine metacognition, or thinking about thinking. These and other abilities present in other species to at most a small degree are not necessarily embraced by the core knowledge approach.

The several theories of human cognitive uniqueness outlined here have all been proposed within just the last few years, so it will not be surprising if new proposals and refinements of old ones continue to surface. Even more likely, what appears uniquely human today may not be accepted as such tomorrow, and vice versa. As we have seen, the recent history of research on comparative cognition is one of continual appearance of evidence for unexpectedly humanlike abilities in other species (and occasionally for unexpectedly animal-like behavior in humans), followed by challenges, refinements, almost always a more nuanced and qualified view. We have seen examples of the importance of species or even population differences, the ubiquitous influence of contextual variables, and the need for multiple tests of what may seem to human experimenters a unitary capacity. In short, as in any rich and vibrant scientific field, understanding is continually evolving. Long may it continue to!

Suggestions for Further Reading

Barrett, H. C., & Kurzban, R. (2006). Modularity in cognition: Framing the debate. *Psychological Review, 113*, 628–647.

Carey, S. (2011). Precis of The Origin of Concepts. *Behavioral and Brain Sciences, 34*, 113–167.

Penn, D. C., Holyoak, K. J., & Povinelli, D. J. (2008). Darwin's mistake: Explaining the discontinuity between human and nonhuman minds. *Behavioral and Brain Sciences, 31*, 109–178.

Premack, D. (2007). Human and animal cognition: Continuity and discontinuity. *Proceedings of the National Academy of Sciences USA, 104*, 13861–13867.

Shettleworth, S. J. (2010). Clever animals and killjoy explanations in comparative psychology. *Trends in Cognitive Sciences, 14*, 477–481.

Tomasello, M., Carpenter, M., Call, J., Behne, T., & Moll, H. (2005). Understanding and sharing intentions: The origins of cultural cognition. *The Behavioral and Brain Sciences, 28*, 675–735.

REFERENCES

....

Addis, D. R., Wong, A. T., & Schacter, D. L. (2007). Remembering the past and imagining the future: Common and distinct neural substrates during event construction and elaboration. *Neuropsychologia*, *45*, 1363–1377.

Amici, F., Aureli, F., & Call, J. (2008). Fission–fusion dynamics, behavioral flexibility, and inhibitory control in primates. *Current Biology*, *18*, 1415–1419.

Amici, F., Aureli, F., Visalberghi, E., & Call, J. (2009). Spider monkeys (*Ateles geoffroyi*) and capuchin monkeys (*Cebus apella*) follow gaze around barriers: Evidence for perspective taking? *Journal of Comparative Psychology*, *123*, 368–374.

Apperly, I. A., & Butterfill, S. A. (2009). Do humans have two systems to track beliefs and belief-like states? *Psychological Review*, *116*, 953–970.

Babb, S. J., & Crystal, J. D. (2005). Discrimination of what, when, and where: Implications for episodic-like memory in rats. *Learning and Motivation*, *36*, 177–189.

Balda, R. P., & Kamil, A. C. (2006). Linking life zones, life history traits, ecology, and spatial cognition in four allopatric southwestern seed caching corvids. In M.F. Brown and R.G. Cook (Eds.), *Animal Spatial Cognition: Comparative, Neural, and Computational Approaches*. [On-line]. Available: www.pigeon.psy.tufts.edu/asc/Balda.

Balsam, P. D., & Gallistel, C. R. (2009). Temporal maps and informativeness in associative learning. *Trends in Neurosciences*, *32*, 73–78.

Barrett, H. C., & Kurzban, R. (2006). Modularity in cognition: Framing the debate. *Psychological Review*, *113*, 628–647.

Basile, B. M., & Hampton, R. R. (2011). Monkeys recall and reproduce simple shapes from memory. *Current Biology*, *21*, 774–778.

Bateson, P., & Mameli, M. (2007). The innate and the acquired: Useful clusters or a residual distinction from folk biology? *Developmental Psychobiology*, *49*, 818–831.

Beck, S. R., Apperly, I. A., Chappell, J., Guthrie, C., & Cutting, N. (2011). Making tools isn't child's play. *Cognition*, *119*, 301–306.

Bentley–Condit, V. K., & Smith, E. O. (2010). Animal tool use: Current definitions and an updated comprehensive catalog. *Behaviour*, *147*, 185–221.

Bergman, T. J., Beehner, J. C., Cheney, D. L., & Seyfarth, R. M. (2003). Hierarchical classification by rank and kinship in baboons. *Science*, *302*, 1234–1236.

Bhatt, R. S., Wasserman, E. A., Reynolds, W. F. J., & Knauss, K. S. (1988). Conceptual behavior in pigeons: Categorization of both familiar and novel examples from four classes of natural and artificial stimuli. *Journal of Experimental Psychology: Animal Behavior Processes*, *14*, 219–234.

Bingman, V. P., & Cheng, K. (2005). Mechanisms of animal global navigation: Comparative perspectives and enduring challenges. *Ethology, Ecology & Evolution*, *17*, 295–318.

Bird, C. D., & Emery, N. J. (2009). Insightful problem solving and creative tool modification by captive nontool–using rooks. *Proceedings of the National Academy of Sciences USA*, *106*, 10370–10375.

Bitterman, M. E. (1975). The comparative analysis of learning. *Science*, *188*, 699–709.

Blough, D. S. (2006). Reaction-time explorations of visual perception, attention, and decision in pigeons. In E. A. Wasserman & T. R. Zentall (Eds.), *Comparative Cognition: Experimental Exploration of Animal Intelligence* (pp. 77–93). New York: Oxford University Press.

Bluff, L. A., Troscianko, J., Weir, A. A. S., Kacelnik, A., & Rutz, C. (2010). Tool use by wild New Caledonian crows *Corvus moneduloides* at natural foraging sites. *Proceedings of the Royal Society of London B*, *277*, 1377–1385.

Bluff, L. A., Weir, A. A. S., Rutz, C., Wimpenny, J. H., & Kacelnik, A. (2007). Tool-related cognition in New Caledonian crows. *Comparative Cognition & Behavior Reviews*, *2*, 1–25.

Boakes, R. (1984). *From Darwin to Behaviourism*. Cambridge, England: Cambridge University Press.

Boesch, C. (2007). What makes us human (*Homo sapiens*)? The challenge of cognitive cross–species comparison. *Journal of Comparative Psychology*, *121*, 227–240.

Boesch, C., & Boesch–Acherman, H. (2000). *The Chimpanzees of the Tai Forest*. Oxford, England: Oxford University Press.

Bolhuis, J., & Verhulst, S. (Eds.). (2009). *Tinbergen's Legacy: Function and Mechanism in Behavioral Biology*. Cambridge, England: Cambridge University Press.

Bolhuis, J. J., & Macphail, E. M. (2001). A critique of the neuroecology of learning and memory. *Trends in Cognitive Sciences*, 5, 426–433.

Bolhuis, J. J., Okanoya, K., & Scharff, C. (2010). Twitter evolution: Converging mechanisms in birdsong and human speech. *Nature Reviews Neuroscience*, 11, 747–759.

Bond, A. B. (2007). The evolution of color polymorphism: Crypticity, searching images, and apostatic selection. *Annual Review of Ecology, Evolution, and Systematics*, 38, 489–514.

Bond, A. B., Wei, C. A., & Kamil, A. C. (2010). Cognitive representation in transitive inference: A comparison of four corvid species. *Behavioural Processes*, 85, 283–292.

Bouton, M. E. (2007). *Learning and Behavior*. Sunderland, MA: Sinauer Associates.

Bouton, M. E., & Moody, E. W. (2004). Memory processes in classical conditioning. *Neuroscience and Biobehavioral Reviews*, 28, 663–674.

Briscoe, A. D., & Chittka, L. (2001). The evolution of color vision in insects. *Annual Review of Entomology*, 46, 471–510.

Brosnan, S. F., & de Waal, F. B. M. (2003). Monkeys reject unequal pay. *Nature*, 425, 297–299.

Brosnan, S. F., Parrish, A., Beran, M. J., Flemming, T., Heimbauer, L., Talbot, C. F., et al. (2011). Responses to the assurance game in monkeys, apes, and humans using equivalent procedures. *Proceedings of the National Academy of Sciences USA*, 108, 3442–3447.

Brosnan, S. F., Talbot, C., Ahlgren, M., Lambeth, S. P., & Schapiro, S. J. (2010). Mechanisms underlying responses to unequitable outcomes in chimpanzees, *Pan troglodytes*. *Animal Behaviour*, 79, 1229–1237.

Brown, A. L. (1990). Domain-specific principles affect learning and transfer in children. *Cognitive Science*, 14, 107–133.

Bshary, R., & d'Souza, A. (2005). Cooperation in communication networks: Indirect reciprocity in interactions between cleaner fish and client reef fish. In P. K. McGregor (Ed.), *Animal Communication Networks* (pp. 521–539). Cambridge, England: Cambridge University Press.

Bugnyar, T., & Heinrich, B. (2005). Ravens, *Corvis corax*, differentiate between knowledgeable and ignorant competitors. *Proceedings of the Royal Society B*, 272, 1641–1646.

Buhusi, C. V., & Meck, W. H. (2005). What makes us tick? Functional and neural mechanisms of interval timing. *Nature Reviews Neuroscience*, 6, 755–765.

Buller, D. J. (2005). Evolutionary psychology: The emperor's new paradigm. *Trends in Cognitive Sciences*, 9, 277–283.

Burkhardt, R. W. (2005). *Patterns of Behavior*. Chicago, IL: University of Chicago Press.

Byrne, R., & Bates, L. A. (2010). Primate social cognition: Uniquely primate, uniquely social, or just unique? *Neuron*, *65*, 815–830.

Call, J. (2010). Do apes know they could be wrong? *Animal Cognition*, *13*, 689–700.

Call, J., & Carpenter, M. (2001). Do apes and children know what they have seen? *Animal Cognition*, *4*, 207–220.

Call, J., & Tomasello, M. (2008). Does the chimpanzee have a theory of mind? 30 years later. *Trends in Cognitive Sciences*, *12*, 187–192.

Cantlon, J. F., & Brannon, E. M. (2006). Shared system for ordering small and large numbers in monkeys and humans. *Psychological Science*, *17*, 401–406.

Cantlon, J. F., Platt, M. L., & Brannon, E. M. (2009). Beyond the number domain. *Trends in Cognitive Sciences*, *13*, 83–89.

Carey, S. (2009). *The Origin of Concepts*. New York: Oxford University Press.

Carey, S. (2011). Precis of The Origin of Concepts. *Behavioral and Brain Sciences*, *34*, 113–167.

Caro, T. M., & Hauser, M. D. (1992). Is there teaching in nonhuman animals? *The Quarterly Review of Biology*, *67*, 151–174.

Carroll, S. B. (2005). *Endless Forms Most Beautiful*. New York: W.W. Norton and Company.

Carruthers, P. (2008). Meta-cognition in animals: A skeptical look. *Mind & Language*, *23*, 58–89.

Catmur, C., Walsh, V., & Heyes, C. (2009). Associative sequence learning: The role of experience in the development of imitation and the mirror system. *Philosophical Transactions of the Royal Society B*, *364*, 2369–2380.

Cheney, D. L. (2011). Cooperation and cognition. In R. Menzel & J. Fischer (Eds.), *Animal Thinking: Contemporary Issues in Comparative Cognition* (pp. 239–252). Cambridge, MA: MIT Press.

Cheney, D. L., & Seyfarth, R. M. (2005a). Social complexity and the information acquired during eavesdropping by primates and other animals. In P. K. McGregor (Ed.), *Animal Communication Networks* (pp. 583–603). Cambridge, England: Cambridge University Press.

Cheney, D. L., & Seyfarth, R. M. (2005b). Constraints and preadaptations in the earliest stages of language evolution. *The Linguistic Review*, *22*, 135–159.

Cheney, D. L., & Seyfarth, R. M. (2007). *Baboon Metaphysics: The Evolution of a Social Mind*. Chicago, IL: University of Chicago Press.

Cheng, K. (1986). A purely geometric module in the rat's spatial representation. *Cognition*, *23*, 149–178.

Cheng, K., & Newcombe, N. S. (2005). Is there a geometric module for spatial orientation? Squaring theory and evidence. *Psychonomic Bulletin & Review*, *12*, 1–23.

Cheng, K., Shettleworth, S. J., Huttenlocher, J., & Rieser, J. J. (2007). Bayesian integration of spatial information. *Psychological Bulletin, 133*, 625–637.

Cheng, K., & Wignall, A. E. (2006). Honeybees (*Apis mellifera*) holding on to memories: Response competition causes retroactive interference effects. *Animal Cognition, 9*, 141–150.

Cheung, A., Stürzl, W., Zeil, J., & Cheng, K. (2008). The information content of panoramic images II: View-based navigation in nonrectangular experimental arenas. *Journal of Experimental Psychology: Animal Behavior Processes, 34*, 15–30.

Church, R. M. (2002). Temporal learning. In C. R. Gallistel (Ed.), *Stevens' Handbook of Experimental Psychology* (Vol. 3, pp. 365–393). New York: John Wiley & Sons, Inc.

Church, R. M. (2006). Behavioristic. cognitive, biological, and quantitative explanations of timing. In E. A. Wasserman & T. R. Zentall (Eds.), *Comparative Cognition: Experimental Explorations of Animal Intelligence* (pp. 249–269). New York: Oxford University Press.

Clayton, N. S., & Dickinson, A. (1998). Episodic-like memory during cache recovery by scrub jays. *Nature, 395*, 272–274.

Clutton-Brock, T. H. (2009). Cooperation between non-kin in animal societies. *Nature, 462*, 51–57.

Coltheart, M. (1999). Modularity and cognition. *Trends in Cognitive Sciences, 3*, 115–120.

Cook, R. G. (Ed.). (2001). *Avian Visual Cognition*. [On-line]. Available: www.pigeon.psy.tufts.edu/avc/.

Cook, R. G., Levison, D. G., Gillett, S. R., & Blaisdell, A. P. (2005). Capacity and limits of associative memory in pigeons. *Psychonomic Bulletin & Review, 12*, 350–358.

Cook, R. G., & Smith, J. D. (2006). Stages of abstraction and exemplar memorization in pigeon category learning. *Psychological Science, 17*, 1059–1067.

Corballis, M. C. (2007). Recursion, language, and starlings. *Cognitive Science, 31*, 697–704.

Corballis, M. C. (2011). *The Recursive Mind*. Princeton, NJ: Princeton University Press.

Cordes, S., & Brannon, E. M. (2008). Quantitative competencies in infancy. *Developmental Science, 11*, 803–808.

Correia, S. P. C., Dickinson, A., & Clayton, N. S. (2007). Western scrub-jays anticipate future needs independently of their current motivational state. *Current Biology, 17*, 856–861.

Cosmides, L. (1989). The logic of social exchange: Has natural selection shaped how humans reason? Studies with the Wason selection task. *Cognition, 31*, 187–276.

Cosmides, L., & Tooby, J. (1994). Origins of domain specificity: The evolution of functional organization. In L. A. Hirschfeld & S. A. Gelman (Eds.), *Mapping the Mind* (pp. 85–116). Cambridge, England: Cambridge University Press.

Couzin, I. D. (2009). Collective cognition in animal groups. *Trends in Cognitive Sciences, 13,* 36–43.

Crystal, J. D. (2006). Sensitivity to time: Implications for the representation of time. In E. A. Wasserman & T. R. Zentall (Eds.), *Comparative Cognition: Experimental Explorations of Animal Intelligence* (pp. 270–284). New York: Oxford University Press.

Crystal, J. D. (2009). Elements of episodic-like memory in animal models. *Behavioural Processes, 80,* 269–277.

Curio, E. (1988). Cultural transmission of enemy recognition by birds. In T. R. Zentall & B. G. Galef, Jr. (Eds.), *Social Learning: Psychological and Biological Perspectives* (pp. 75–97). Hillsdale, NJ: Erlbaum.

Cuthill, I. C., Partridge, J. C., Bennett, A. T. D., Church, S. C., Hart, N. S., & Hunt, S. (2000). Ultraviolet vision in birds. *Advances in the Study of Behavior, 29,* 159–214.

Dally, J. M., Emery, N. J., & Clayton, N. S. (2006). Food-caching western scrub-jays keep track of who was watching when. *Science, 312,* 1662–1665.

Darwin, C. (1859). *On the Origin of Species.* London: John Murray.

Darwin, C. (1871). *The Descent of Man and Selection in Relation to Sex.* London: John Murray.

Darwin, C. (1879/2004). *The Descent of Man and Selection in Relation to Sex* (2nd ed.). London: Penguin.

Dawkins, M. S. (2006). A user's guide to animal welfare science. *Trends in Ecology and Evolution, 21,* 77–82.

De Houwer, J. (2009). The propositional approach to associative learning as an alternative for association formation models. *Learning & Behavior, 37,* 1–20.

de Kort, S. R., Dickinson, A., & Clayton, N. S. (2005). Retrospective cognition by food-caching western scrub-jays. *Learning and Motivation, 36,* 159–176.

de Waal, F. B. M. (2008). Putting the altruism back into altruism: The evolution of empathy. *Annual Review of Psychology, 59,* 279–300.

de Waal, F. B. M., & Tyack, P. L. (Eds.). (2003). *Animal Social Complexity.* Cambridge, MA: Harvard University Press.

Dennett, D. C. (1983). Intentional systems in cognitive ethology: The "Panglossian paradigm" defended. *The Behavioral and Brain Sciences, 6,* 343–390.

Dickinson, A. (2008). Why a rat is not a beast machine. In M. Davies & L. Weiskrantz (Eds.), *Frontiers of Consciousness* (pp. 275–288). Oxford, England: Oxford University Press.

Dickinson, A. (2011). Goal-directed behaviour and future planning in animals. In R. Menzel & J. Fischer (Eds.), *Animal Thinking: Contemporary Issues in Comparative Cognition* (pp. 79–91). Cambridge, MA: MIT Press.

Dickinson, A., & Balleine, B. (2002). The role of learning in the operation of motivational systems. In C. R. Gallistel (Ed.), *Stevens' Handbook of Experimental Psychology* (3rd ed., Vol. 3, pp. 497–533). New York: John Wiley & Sons.

Doeller, C. F., & Burgess, N. (2008). Distinct error-correcting and incidental learning of location relative to landmarks and boundaries. *Proceedings of the National Academy of Sciences USA, 105,* 5909–5914.

Donaldson, M. C., Lachmann, M., & Bergstrom, C. T. (2007). The evolution of functionally referential meaning in a structured world. *Journal of Theoretical Biology, 246,* 225–233.

Dong, S., & Clayton, D. F. (2009). Habituation in songbirds. *Neurobiology of Learning and Memory, 92,* 183–188.

Dukas, R. (2004). Causes and consequences of limited attention. *Brain Behavior and Evolution, 63,* 197–210.

Dukas, R., & Kamil, A. C. (2000). The cost of limited attention in blue jays. *Behavioral Ecology, 11,* 502–506.

Dukas, R., & Ratcliffe, J. M. (Eds.). (2009). *Cognitive Ecology II.* Chicago, IL: The University of Chicago Press.

Dunbar, R. I. M., & Shultz, S. (2007). Evolution in the social brain. *Science, 317,* 1344–1347.

Dunlap, J. C., Loros, J. J., & Decoursey, P. J. (Eds.). (2003). *Chronobiology: Biological Timekeeping.* Sunderland, MA: Sinauer Associates Inc.

Dyer, F. C. (1991). Bees acquire route-based memories but not cognitive maps in a familiar landscape. *Animal Behaviour, 41,* 239–246.

Dyer, F. C. (2002). The biology of the dance language. *Annual Review of Entomology, 47,* 917–949.

Eacott, M. J., & Easton, A. (2010). Episodic memory in animals: Remembering which occasion. *Neuropsychologia, 48,* 2273–2280.

Eacott, M. J., & Norman, G. (2004). Integrated memory for object, place, and context in rats: A possible model of episodic-like memory? *Journal of Neuroscience, 24,* 1948–1953.

Eichenbaum, H., & Fortin, N. J. (2009). The neurobiology of memory based predictions. *Philosophical Transactions of the Royal Society B: Biological Sciences, 364,* 1183–1191.

Eichenbaum, H., Fortin, N. J., Ergorul, C., Wright, S. P., & Agster, K. L. (2005). Episodic recollection in animals: "If it walks like a duck and quacks like a duck…" *Learning and Motivation, 36,* 190–207.

Emery, N. J. (2000). The eyes have it: The neuroethology, function and evolution of social gaze. *Neuroscience and Biobehavioral Reviews, 24,* 581–604.

Emery, N. J., & Clayton, N. S. (2009a). Comparative social cognition. *Annual Review of Psychology, 60*, 87–113.

Emery, N. J., & Clayton, N. S. (2009b). Tool use and physical cognition in birds and mammals. *Current Opinion in Neurobiology, 19*, 27–33.

Emery, N. J., Clayton, N. S., & Frith, C. (Eds.). (2007). *Social Intelligence: From Brain to Culture*. Oxford, England: Oxford University Press.

Endler, J. A., Westcott, D. A., Madden, J. R., & Robson, T. (2005). Animal visual systems and the evolution of color patterns: Sensory processing illuminates signal evolution. *Evolution, 59*, 1795–1818.

Epstein, R. (1985). Animal cognition as the praxist views it. *Neuroscience and Biobehavioral Reviews, 9*, 623–630.

Epstein, R., Kirshnit, C. E., Lanza, R. P., & Rubin, L. C. (1984). "Insight" in the pigeon: Antecedents and determinants of an intelligent performance. *Nature, 308*, 61–62.

Ernard, W., & Pääbo, S. (2004). Comparative primate genomics. *Annual Review of Genomics and Human Genetics, 5*, 351–378.

Etienne, A. S. (2003). How does path integration interact with olfaction, vision, and the representation of space? In K. J. Jeffery (Ed.), *The Neurobiology of Spatial Behaviour* (pp. 48–66). Oxford, England: Oxford University Press.

Etienne, A. S., & Jeffery, K. J. (2004). Path integration in mammals. *Hippocampus, 14*, 180–192.

Evans, C. S., Evans, L., & Marler, P. (1993). On the meaning of alarm calls: Functional reference in an avian vocal system. *Animal Behaviour, 46*, 23–38.

Evans, C. S., & Marler, P. (1994). Food calling and audience effects in male chickens, *Gallus gallus*: Their relationships to food availability, courtship and social facilitation. *Animal Behaviour, 47*, 1159–1170.

Evans, J. S. B. T. (2002). Logic and human reasoning: An assessment of the deduction paradigm. *Psychological Bulletin, 128*, 978–996.

Fagot, J., & Cook, R. G. (2006). Evidence for large long-term memory capacities in baboons and pigeons and its implications for learning and the evolution of cognition. *Proceedings of the National Academy of Sciences USA, 103*, 17564–17567.

Feeney, M. C., Roberts, W. A., & Sherry, D. F. (2011). Black-capped chickadees *(Poecile atricapillus)* anticipate future outcomes of foraging choices. *Journal of Experimental Psychology: Animal Behavior Processes, 37*, 30–40.

Finlay, B. L. (2007). Endless minds most beautiful. *Developmental Science, 10*, 30–34.

Fitch, W. T. (2005). The evolution of language: A comparative review. *Biology and Philosophy, 20*, 193–230.

Fitch, W. T. (2010). *The Evolution of Language*. Cambridge, England: Cambridge University Press.

Flemming, T. M., Thompson, R. K. R., Beran, M. J., & Washburn, D. A. (2011). Analogical reasoning and the differential outcome effect: Transitory bridging of the conceptual gap for Rhesus monkeys (*Maccaca mulatta*). *Journal of Experimental Psychology: Animal Behavior Processes, 37*, 353–360.

Fodor, J. A. (1983). *The Modularity of Mind*. Cambridge, MA: MIT Press.

Frank, M. J., Rudy, J. W., Levy, W. B., & O'Reily, R. C. (2005). When logic fails: Implicit transitive inference in humans. *Memory & Cognition, 33*, 742–750.

Franks, N. R., & Richardson, T. (2006). Teaching in tandem-running ants. *Nature, 439*, 153.

Furrer, R. D., & Manser, M. B. (2009). The evolution of urgency-based and functionally referential alarm calls in ground-dwelling species. *The American Naturalist, 173*, 400-410.

Galef, B. G. (2007). Social learning by rodents. In J. O. Wolff & P. W. Sherman (Eds.), *Rodent Societies* (pp. 207–215). Chicago, IL: University of Chicago Press.

Galef, B. G. (2009 a). Strategies for social learning: Testing predictions from formal theory. *Advances in the Study of Behavior, 39*, 117– 151.

Galef, B. G. (2009 b). Culture in animals? In K. N. Laland & B. G. Galef, Jr. (Eds.), *The Question of Animal Culture* (pp. 222–246). Cambridge, MA: Harvard University Press.

Gallistel, C. R. (1990). *The Organization of Learning*. Cambridge, MA: MIT Press.

Gallistel, C. R. (1999). The replacement of general-purpose learning models with adaptively specialized learning modules. In M. Gazziniga (Ed.), *The Cognitive Neurosciences* (pp. 1179–1191). Cambridge, MA: MIT Press.

Gelman, R. (2009). Learning in core and noncore domains. In L. Tommasi, M. A. Peterson, & L. Nadel (Eds.), *Cognitive Biology* (pp. 247–260). Cambridge, MA: MIT Press.

Gergely, G., Nádasdy, Z., Csibra, G., & Bíró, S. (1995). Taking the intentional stance at 12 months of age. *Cognition, 56*, 165–193.

Ghirlanda, S., & Enquist, M. (2003). A century of generalization. *Animal Behaviour, 66*, 15–36.

Gibbon, J., & Church, R. M. (1990). Representation of time. *Cognition, 37*, 23–54.

Gibbon, J., Church, R. M., Fairhurst, S., & Kacelnik, A. (1988). Scalar expectancy theory and choice between delayed rewards. *Psychological Review, 95*, 102–114.

Gibson, B. M. (2001). Cognitive maps not used by humans (*Homo sapiens*) during a dynamic navigational task. *Journal of Comparative Psychology, 115*, 397–402.

Gigerenzer, G. (1997). The modularity of social intelligence. In A. Whiten & R. W. Byrne (Eds.), *Machiavellian Intelligence II: Extensions and Evaluation* (pp. 264–288). Cambridge, England: Cambridge University Press.

Girndt, A., Meier, T., & Call, J. (2008). Task constraints mask great apes' ability to solve the trap-table task. *Journal of Experimental Psychology: Animal Behavior Processes, 34*, 54–62.

Glimcher, P. W., & Rustichini, A. (2004). Neuroeconomics: The consilience of brain and decision. *Science, 306*, 447–452.

Grant, D. S. (1976). Effect of sample presentation time on long-delay matching in pigeons. *Learning and Motivation, 7*, 580–590.

Grant, P. R., & Grant, B. R. (2008). *How and Why Species Multiply*. Princeton, NJ: Princeton University Press.

Griffin, D. R. (1978). Prospects for a cognitive ethology. *The Behavioral and Brain Sciences, 4*, 527–538.

Grosenick, L., Clement, T. S., & Fernald, R. D. (2007). Fish can infer social rank by observation alone. *Nature, 445*, 429–432.

Grüter, C., & Farina, W. M. (2009). The honeybee waggle dance: Can we follow the steps? *Trends in Ecology and Evolution, 24*, 242–247.

Hampton, R. R. (2001). Rhesus monkeys know when they remember. *Proceedings of the National Academy of Sciences USA, 98*, 5359–5362.

Hampton, R. R. (2009). Multiple demonstrations of metacognition in nonhumans: Converging evidence or multiple mechanisms? *Comparative Cognition & Behavior Reviews, 4*, 17–28.

Hampton, R. R., Zivin, A., & Murray, E. A. (2004). Rhesus monkeys (*Macaca mulatta*) discriminate between knowing and not knowing and collect information as needed before acting. *Animal Cognition, 7*, 239–246.

Hansell, M., & Ruxton, G. D. (2008). Setting animal tool use within the context of animal construction behavior. *Trends in Ecology and Evolution, 23*, 73–78.

Hanson, H. M. (1959). Effects of discrimination training on stimulus generalization. *Journal of Experimental Psychology, 58*, 321–334.

Hare, B., Call, J., Agnetta, B., & Tomasello, M. (2000). Chimpanzees know what conspecifics do and do not see. *Animal Behaviour, 59*, 771–785.

Harper, D. N., McLean, A. P., & Dalrymple-Alford, J. C. (1993). List item memory in rats: Effects of delay and delay task. *Journal of Experimental Psychology: Animal Behavior Processes, 19*, 307–316.

Hauser, M. D., Carey, S., & Hauser, L. B. (2000). Spontaneous number representation in semi-free-ranging rhesus monkeys. *Proceedings of the Royal Society of London B, 267*, 829–833.

Hauser, M. D., Chomsky, N., & Fitch, W. T. (2002). The faculty of language: What is it, who has it, and how did it evolve? *Science, 298*, 1569–1579.

Hauser, M. D., Kralik, J., & Botto-Mahan, C. (1999). Problem solving and functional design features: Experiments on cotton-top tamarins, *Saguinus oedipus oedipus*. *Animal Behaviour, 57*, 565–582.

Healy, S. D., & Rowe, C. (2007). A critique of comparative studies of brain size. *Proceeding of the Royal Society of London B, 274*, 453–464.

Hemelrijk, C. (2011). Simple reactions to nearby neighbors and complex social behavior in primates. In R. Menzel & J. Fischer (Eds.), *Animal Thinking: Contemporary Issues in Comparative Cognition* (pp. 223–238). Cambridge, MA: MIT Press.

Henderson, J., Hurly, T. A., Bateson, M., & Healy, S. D. (2006). Timing in free-living rufous hummingbirds, *Selasphorus rufus*. *Current Biology, 16*, 512–515.

Herman, L. M., & Uyeyama, R. K. (1999). The dolphin's grammatical competency: Comments on Kako (1999). *Animal Learning & Behavior, 27*, 18–23.

Herrmann, E., Call, J., Hernández-Lloreda, M. V., Hare, B., & Tomasello, M. (2007). Humans have evolved specialized skills of social cognition: The cultural intelligence hypothesis. *Science, 317*, 1360–1366.

Herrmann, E., Hernandez-Lloreda, M. V., Call, J., Hare, B., & Tomasello, M. (2010). The structure of individual differences in the cognitive abilities of children and chimpanzees. *Psychological Science, 21*, 102–110.

Herrnstein, R. J., Loveland, D. H., & Cable, C. (1976). Natural concepts in pigeons. *Journal of Experimental Psychology: Animal Behavior Processes, 2*, 285–311.

Heyes, C. (2008). Beast Machines? Questions of animal consciousness. In M. Davies & L. Weiskrantz (Eds.), *Frontiers of Consciousness* (pp. 259–274). Oxford, England: Oxford University Press.

Heyes, C. (2009). Evolution, development, and intentional control of imitation. *Philosophical Transactions of the Royal Society B, 364*, 2293–2298.

Heyes, C. (2010). Where do mirror neurons come from? *Neuroscience and Biobehavioral Reviews, 34*, 575–583.

Heyes, C. M. (1998). Theory of mind in nonhuman primates. *Behavioral and Brain Sciences, 21*, 101–148.

Holekamp, K. E., Sakai, S. T., & Lundrigan, B. L. (2007). Social intelligence in the spotted hyena (*Crocuta crocuta*). *Philosophical Transactions of the Royal Society B, 362*, 523–538.

Holmes, W. G., & Mateo, J. M. (2007). Kin recognition in rodents: Issues and evidence. In J. O. Wolff & P. W. Sherman (Eds.), *Rodent Societies: An Ecological & Evolutionary Perspective* (pp. 216–228). Chicago, IL: The University of Chicago Press.

Holzhaider, J. C., Hunt, G. R., & Gray, R. D. (2010). Social learning in New Caledonian crows. *Learning & Behavior, 38*, 206–219.

Hopper, L. M. (2010). "Ghost" experiments and the dissection of social learning in humans and animals. *Biological Reviews, 85*, 685–701.

Hoppitt, W., & Laland, K. (2008). Social processes influencing learning in animals. *Advances in the Study of Behavior, 38*, 105–165.

Hoppitt, W. J. E., Brown, G. R., Kendal, R., Rendell, L., Thornton, A., Webster, M. M., et al. (2008). Lessons from animal teaching. *Trends in Ecology and Evolution, 23*, 486–493.

Horner, V., Carter, J. D., Suchak, M., & de Waal, F. B. M. (2011). Spontaneous prosocial choice by chimpanzees. *Proceedings of the National Academy of Sciences USA, 108*, 13847–13851.

Hulse, S. H., Fowler, H., & Honig, W. K. (Eds.). (1978). *Cognitive Processes in Animal Behavior*. Hillsdale, NJ: Erlbaum.

Humle, T., & Matsuzawa, T. (2002). Ant-dipping among the chimpanzees of Bossou, Guinea, and some comparisons with other sites. *American Journal of Primatology, 58*, 133–148.

Humphrey, N. K. (1976). The social function of intellect. In P. P. G. Bateson & R. A. Hinde (Eds.), *Growing Points in Ethology* (pp. 303–317). Cambridge, England: Cambridge University Press.

Hunt, G. R. (1996). Manufacture and use of hook-tools by New Caledonian crows. *Nature, 379*, 249–251.

Hunter, W. S. (1913). The delayed reaction in animals and children. *Behavior Monographs, 2*.

Iacoboni, M. (2009). Imitation, empathy, and mirror neurons. *Annual Review of Psychology, 60*, 653–670.

Janson, C. H., & Byrne, R. (2007). What wild primates know about resources: Opening up the black box. *Animal Cognition, 10*, 357–367.

Jeffery, K. J. (2010). Theoretical accounts of spatial learning: A neurobiological view (commentary on Pearce, 2009). *Quarterly Journal of Experimental Psychology, 63*, 1683–1699.

Jensen, K., Call, J., & Tomasello, M. (2007). Chimpanzees are rational maximizers in an ultimatum game. *Science, 318*, 107–109.

Jolly, A. (1966). Lemur social behavior and primate intelligence. *Science, 153*, 501–506.

Jozefowiez, J., Staddon, J. E. R., & Cerutti, D. T. (2009). Metacognition in animals: How do we know that they know? *Comparative Cognition & Behavior Reviews, 4*, 29–39.

Kacelnik, A. (2006). Meanings of rationality. In S. Hurley & M. Nudds (Eds.), *Rational Animals?* (pp. 87–106). Oxford, England: Oxford University Press.

Kadosh, R. C., Lammertyn, J., & Izard, V. (2008). Are numbers special? An overview of chronometric, neuroimaging, developmental and comparative studies of magnitude representation. *Progress in Neurobiology, 84*, 132–147.

Kako, E. (1999). Elements of syntax in the systems of three language-trained animals. *Animal Learning & Behavior, 27*, 1–14.

Kamil, A. C. (1988). A synthetic approach to the study of animal intelligence. In D. W. Leger (Ed.), *Comparative Perspectives in Modern Psychology: Nebraska Symposium on Motivation* (Vol. 35, pp. 230–257). Lincoln, NE: University of Nebraska Press.

Kamil, A. C., & Cheng, K. (2001). Way-finding and landmarks: The multiple bearings hypothesis. *Journal of Experimental Biology, 204*, 103–113.

Karakashian, S. J., Gyger, M., & Marler, P. (1988). Audience effects on alarm calling in chickens (*Gallus gallus*). *Journal of Comparative Psychology, 102*, 129–135.

Kastak, C. R., & Schusterman, R. J. (2002). Sea lions and equivalence: Expanding classes by exclusion. *Journal of the Experimental Analysis of Behavior, 78*, 449–465.

Kendal, R. L., Galef, B. G., & van Schaik, C. P. (2010). Social learning research outside the laboratory: How and why? *Learning & Behavior, 38*, 187–194.

Kohler, W. (1925/1959). *The Mentality of Apes* (E. Winter, Trans.). New York: Vintage Books.

Kornell, N., Son, L. M., & Terrace, H. S. (2007). Transfer of metacognitive skills and hint-seeking in monkeys. *Psychological Science, 18*, 64–71.

Kounios, J., & Beeman, M. (2009). The *Aha!* moment. *Current Directions in Psychological Science, 18*, 210–216.

Laland, K. N., Atton, N., & Webster, M. M. (2011). From fish to fashion: Experimental and theoretical insights into the evolution of culture. *Philosophical Transactions of the Royal Society B, 366*, 958–968.

Laland, K. N., & Galef, B. G. (Eds.). (2009). *The Question of Animal Culture.* Cambridge, MA: Harvard University Press.

Landau, B., & Lakusta, L. (2009). Spatial representation across species: geometry, language, and maps. *Current Opinion in Neurobiology, 19*, 12–19.

Lea, S. E. G., & Wills, A. J. (2008). Use of multiple dimensions in learned discriminations. *Comparative Cognition & Behavior Reviews, 3*, 115–133.

Lefebvre, L., & Sol, D. (2008). Brains, lifestyles and cognition: Are there general trends? *Brain Behavior and Evolution, 72*, 135–144.

Leslie, A. M., Gelman, R., & Gallistel, C. R. (2008). The generative basis of natural number concepts. *Trends in Cognitive Sciences, 12*, 213–218.

Loretto, M-C., Schloegl, C., & Bugnyar, T. (2010). Northern bald ibises follow others' gaze into distance space but not behind barriers. *Biology Letters, 6*, 14–17.

Machado, A. (1997). Learning the temporal dynamics of behavior. *Psychological Review, 104*, 241–265.

Machado, A., & Pata, P. (2005). Testing the scalar expectancy theory (SET) and the learning-to-time model (LeT) in a double bisection task. *Learning & Behavior, 33*, 111–122.

Mackintosh, N. J. (2002). Do not ask whether they have a cognitive map but how they find their way about. *Psicologica, 23*, 165–185.

Macphail, E. M. (1987). The comparative psychology of intelligence. *Behavioral and Brain Sciences, 10*, 645–695.

Manser, M. B. (2009). What do functionally referential alarm calls refer to? In R. Dukas & J. M. Ratcliffe (Eds.), *Cognitive Ecology II* (pp. 229–248). Chicago, IL: University of Chicago Press.

Marler, P., & Peters, S. (1989). Species differences in auditory responsiveness in early vocal learning. In R. J. Dooling & S. H. Hulse (Eds.), *The Comparative Psychology of Audition: Perceiving Complex Sounds* (pp. 243–273). Hillsdale, NJ: Erlbaum.

Marsh, B., Schuck-Paim, C., & Kacelnik, A. (2004). Energetic state during learning affects foraging choices in starlings. *Behavioral Ecology, 15,* 396–399.

Matsuzawa, T. (2009). Symbolic representation of number in chimpanzees. *Current Opinion in Neurobiology, 19,* 92–98.

Matzel, L. D., & Kolata, S. (2010). Selective attention, working memory, and animal intelligence. *Neuroscience and Biobehavioral Reviews, 34,* 23–30.

Maynard Smith, J., & Harper, D. (2003). *Animal Signals.* Oxford, England: Oxford University Press.

McGregor, P. K. (Ed.). (2005). *Animal Communication Networks.* Cambridge, England: Cambridge University Press.

McNaughton, B. L., Battaglia, F. P., Jensen, O., Moser, E. I., & Moser, M. (2006). Path integration and the neural basis of the "cognitive map." *Nature Reviews Neuroscience, 7,* 663–678.

Meck, W. H., & Church, R. M. (1983). A mode control model of counting and timing processes. *Journal of Experimental Psychology: Animal Behavior Processes, 9,* 320–334.

Menzel, R., Greggers, U., Smith, A., Berger, S., Brandt, R., Brunke, S., et al. (2005). Honey bees navigate according to a map-like spatial memory. *Proceedings of the National Academy of Sciences USA, 102,* 3040–3045.

Miller, N. Y., & Shettleworth, S. J. (2007). Learning about environmental geometry: An associative model. *Journal of Experimental Psychology: Animal Behavior Processes, 33,* 191–212.

Mineka, S., & Cook, M. (1988). Social learning and the acquisition of snake fear in monkeys. In T. R. Zentall & B. G. Galef, Jr. (Eds.), *Social Learning: Psychological and Biological Perspectives* (pp. 51–73). Hillsdale, NJ: Erlbaum.

Mobius, Y., Boesch, C., Koops, K., Matsuzawa, T., & Humle, T. (2008). Cultural differences in army ant predation by West African chimpanzees? A comparative study of microecological variables. *Animal Behaviour, 76,* 37–45.

Morgan, C. L. (1894). *An Introduction to Comparative Psychology.* London: Walter Scott.

Mulcahy, N. J., & Call, J. (2006). Apes save tools for future use. *Science, 312,* 1038–1040.

Muller, M., & Wehner, R. (1988). Path integration in desert ants. *Proceedings of the National Academy of Sciences USA, 85,* 5287–5290.

Nagy, M., Akos, Z., Biro, D., & Vicsek, T. (2010). Hierarchical dynamics in pigeon flocks. *Nature, 464,* 890–893.

Newcombe, N. S. (2002). The nativist-empiricist controversy in the context of recent research on spatial and quantitative development. *Psychological Science, 13*, 395–401.

Newcombe, N. S., Ratliff, K. R., Shallcross, W. L., & Twyman, A. (2009). Is cognitive modularity necessary in an evolutionary account of development? In L. Tommasi, M. A. Peterson, & L. Nadel (Eds.), *Cognitive Biology* (pp. 105–126). Cambridge, MA: MIT Press.

Nieder, A., & Dehaene, S. (2009). Representation of number in the brain. *Annual Review of Neuroscience, 32*, 185–208.

Noë, R. (2006). Cooperation experiments: Coordination through communication versus acting apart together. *Animal Behaviour, 71*, 1–18.

Öhman, A., & Mineka, S. (2001). Fears, phobias, and preparedness: Toward an evolved module of fear and fear learning. *Psychological Review, 108*, 483–522.

O'Keefe, J., & Nadel, L. (1978). *The Hippocampus as a Cognitive Map*. Oxford, England: Clarendon Press.

Osiurak, F., Jarry, C., & LeGall, D. (2010). Grasping the affordances, understanding the reasoning: Toward a dialectical theory of human tool use. *Psychological Review, 117*, 517–540.

Osvath, M., & Osvath, H. (2008). Chimpanzee (*Pan troglodytes*) and orangutan (*Pongo abelii*) forethought: Self-control and pre-experience in the face of future tool use. *Animal Cognition, 11*, 661–674.

Ottoni, E. B., & de Resende, B. D. (2005). Watching the best nutcrackers: What capuchin monkeys (*Cebus apella*) know about others' tool-using skills. *Animal Cognition, 24*, 215–219.

Papini, M. R. (2008). *Comparative Psychology* (2nd ed.). New York: Psychology Press.

Paukner, A., Suomi, S. J., Visalberghi, E., & Ferrari, P. F. (2009). Capuchin monkeys display affiliation toward humans who imitate them. *Science, 325*, 880–883.

Paxton, R., Basile, B. M., Adachi, I., Suzuki, W. A., Wilson, M. E., & Hampton, R. R. (2010). Rhesus monkeys (*Macaca mulatta*) rapidly learn to select dominant individuals in videos of artificial social interactions between unfamiliar conspecifics. *Journal of Comparative Psychology, 124*, 395–401.

Paz-y-Mino C., G., Bond, A. B., Kamil, A. C., & Balda, R. P. (2004). Pinyon jays use transitive inference to predict social dominance. *Nature, 430*, 778–781.

Peake, T. M. (2005). Eavesdropping in communication networks. In P. K. McGregor (Ed.), *Animal Communication Networks* (pp. 13–37). Cambridge, England: Cambridge University Press.

Pearce, J. M. (2008). *Animal Learning & Cognition* (3rd ed.). New York: Psychology Press.

Pearce, J. M. (2009). An associative analysis of spatial learning. *Quarterly Journal of Experimental Psychology, 62*, 1665–1684.

Penn, D. C., Holyoak, K. J., & Povinelli, D. J. (2008). Darwin's mistake: Explaining the discontinuity between human and nonhuman minds. *Behavioral and Brain Sciences*, *31*, 109–178.

Penn, D. C., & Povinelli, D. J. (2007). On the lack of evidence that non-human animals possess anything remotely resembling a "theory of mind." *Philosophical Transactions of the Royal Society B*, *362*, 731–744.

Pfungst, O. (1965). *Clever Hans (The Horse of Mr. Von Osten)*. New York: Holt, Rinehart and Winston.

Pica, P., Lemer, C., Izard, V., & Dehaene, S. (2004). Exact and approximate arithmetic in an Amazonian indigene group. *Science*, *306*, 499–503.

Pilley, J. W., & Reid, A. K. (2010). Border collie comprehends object names as verbal referents. *Behavioural Processes*, *86*, 184–195.

Pinker, S., & Jackendoff, R. (2005). The faculty of language: What's special about it? *Cognition*, *95*, 201–236.

Pompilio, L., & Kacelnik, A. (2010). Context-dependent utility overrides absolute memory as a determinant of choice. *Proceedings of the National Academy of Sciences USA*, *107*, 508–512.

Pompilio, L., Kacelnik, A., & Behmer, S. T. (2006). State-dependent learned valuation drives choice in an invertebrate. *Science*, *311*, 1613–1615.

Povinelli, D. J. (2000). *Folk Physics for Apes*. New York: Oxford University Press.

Povinelli, D. J., & Eddy, T. J. (1996). What young chimpanzees know about seeing. *Monographs of the Society for Research in Child Development*, *61*, 1–152.

Povinelli, D. J., & Preuss, T. M. (1995). Theory of mind: Evolutionary history of a cognitive specialization. *Trends in Neurosciences*, *18*, 418–424.

Povinelli, D. J., & Vonk, J. (2004). We don't need a microscope to explore the chimpanzee's mind. *Mind & Language*, *19*, 1–28.

Premack, D. (2007). Human and animal cognition: Continuity and discontinuity. *Proceedings of the National Academy of Sciences USA*, *104*, 13861–13867.

Premack, D. (2010). Why humans are unique: Three theories. *Perspectives on Psychological Science*, *5*, 22–32.

Premack, D., & Woodruff, G. (1978). Does the chimpanzee have a theory of mind? *The Behavioral and Brain Sciences*, *4*, 515–526.

Raby, C. R., Alexis, D. M., Dickinson, A., & Clayton, N. S. (2007). Planning for the future by Western scrub-jays. *Nature*, *445*, 919–921.

Raby, C. R., & Clayton, N. S. (2009). Prospective cognition in animals. *Behavioural Processes*, *80*, 314–324.

Radick, G. (2007). *The Simian Tongue*. Chicago, IL: University of Chicago Press.

Raihani, N. J., & Ridley, A. R. (2008). Experimental evidence for teaching in wild pied babblers. *Animal Behaviour*, *75*, 3–11.

Range, F., Huber, L., & Heyes, C. (2011). Automatic imitation in dogs. *Proceedings of the Royal Society B*, *278*, 211–217.

Reader, S. M., Hager, Y., & Laland, K. N. (2011). The evolution of primate general and cultural intelligence. *Philosophical Transactions of the Royal Society B*, *366*, 1017–1027.

Reid, P. J. (2009). Adapting to the human world: Dogs' responsiveness to our social cues. *Behavioural Processes*, *80*, 325–333.

Reid, P. J., & Shettleworth, S. J. (1992). Detection of cryptic prey: Search image or search rate? *Journal of Experimental Psychology: Animal Behavior Processes, 18,* 273–286.

Rendall, D., Owren, M. J., & Ryan, M. J. (2009). What do animal signals mean? *Animal Behaviour*, *78*, 233–240.

Rendell, L., Fogarty, L., Hoppitt, W. J. E., Morgan, T. J. H., Webster, M. M., & Laland, K. N. (2011). Cognitive culture: Theoretical and empirical insights into social learning strategies. *Trends in Cognitive Sciences*, *15*, 68–78.

Rescorla, R. A. (1988). Pavlovian conditioning: It's not what you think it is. *American Psychologist*, *43*, 151–160.

Rescorla, R. A., & Wagner, A. R. (1972). A theory of Pavlovian conditioning: Variations in the effectiveness of reinforcement and nonreinforcement. In A. H. Black & W. F. Prokasy (Eds.), *Classical Conditioning II: Current Theory and Research* (pp. 64–99). New York: Appleton-Century-Crofts.

Richerson, P. J., & Boyd, R. (2005). *Not by Genes Alone*. Chicago, IL: University of Chicago Press.

Rieucau, G., & Giraldeau, L-A. (2011). Exploring the costs and benefits of social information use: An appraisal of current experimental evidence. *Philosophical Transactions of the Royal Society B*, *366*, 949–957.

Riley, J. R., Greggers, U., Smith, A. D., Reynolds, D. R., & Menzel, R. (2005). The flight paths of honeybees recruited by the waggle dance. *Nature*, *435*, 205–207.

Rizzolatti, G., & Fogassi, L. (2007). Mirror neurons and social cognition. In R. I. M. Dunbar & L. Barrett (Eds.), *The Oxford Handbook of Evolutionary Psychology* (pp. 179–195). Oxford, England: Oxford University Press.

Roberts, S. (1981). Isolation of an internal clock. *Journal of Experimental Psychology: Animal Behavior Processes*, *7*, 242–268.

Roberts, W. A. (2002). Are animals stuck in time? *Psychological Bulletin*, *128*, 473–489.

Roberts, W. A., Cruz, C., & Tremblay, J. (2007). Rats take correct novel routes and shortcuts in an enclosed maze. *Journal of Experimental Psychology: Animal Behavior Processes*, *33*, 79–91.

Roberts, W. A., & Feeney, M. C. (2009). The comparative study of mental time travel. *Trends in Cognitive Sciences*, *13*, 271–277.

Roberts, W. A., Feeney, M. C., MacPherson, K., Petter, M., McMillan, N., & Musolino, E. (2008). Episodic-like memory in rats: Is it based on when or how long ago? *Science*, *320*, 113–115.

Roediger, H. L., Dudai, Y., & Fitzpatrick, S. M. (Eds.). (2007). *Science of Memory: Concepts*. New York: Oxford University Press.

Romanes, G. J. (1892). *Animal Intelligence*. New York: D. Appleton and Company.

Rosati, A. G., & Hare, B. (2009). Looking past the model species: Diversity in gaze-following skills across primates. *Current Opinion in Neurobiology*, *19*, 45–51.

Rosati, A. G., Stevens, J. R., Hare, B., & Hauser, M. D. (2007). The evolutionary origins of human patience: Temporal preferences in chimpanzees, bonobos, and human adults. *Current Biology*, *17*, 1663–1668.

Roth, T. C., Brodin, A., Smulders, T. V., LaDage, L. D., & Pravosudov, V. V. (2010). Is bigger always better? A critical appraisal of the use of volumetric analysis in the study of the hippocampus. *Philosophical Transactions of the Royal Society B*, *365*, 915–931.

Roth, T. C., & Pravosudov, V. V. (2009). Hippocampal volumes and neuron numbers increase along a gradient of environmental harshness: A large-scale comparison. *Proceedings of the Royal Society of London B*, *276*, 401–405.

Ruxton, G. D., Sherratt, T. N., & Speed, M. P. (2004). *Avoiding Attack*. Oxford, England: Oxford University Press.

Santos, L. R., & Hughes, K. D. (2009). Economic cognition in animals and humans: The search for core mechanisms. *Current Opinion in Neurobiology*, *19*, 63–66.

Sanz, C., Morgan, D., & Gulick, S. (2004). New insights into chimpanzees, tools, and termites from the Congo basin. *The American Naturalist*, *164*, 567–581.

Scarf, D., & Colombo, M. (2010). Representation of serial order in pigeons (*Columba livia*). *Journal of Experimental Psychology: Animal Behavior Processes*, *36*, 423–429.

Schino, G., & Aureli, F. (2009). Reciprocal altruism in primates: Partner choice, cognition, and emotions. *Advances in the Study of Behavior*, *39*, 45–69.

Scholl, B. J., & Tremoulet, P. D. (2000). Perceptual causality and animacy. *Trends in Cognitive Sciences*, *4*, 299–309.

Seed, A., & Byrne, R. (2010). Animal tool-use. *Current Biology*, *20*, R1032–R1039.

Seed, A. M., Call, J., Emery, N. J., & Clayton, N. S. (2009). Chimpanzees solve the trap problem when the confound of tool-use is removed. *Journal of Experimental Psychology: Animal Behavior Processes*, *35*, 23–34.

Seed, A. M., Tebbich, S., Emery, N. J., & Clayton, N. S. (2006). Investigating physical cognition in rooks. *Corvus frugilegus*. *Current Biology*, *16*, 697–701.

Seeley, T. D. (1985). *Honey Bee Ecology*. Princeton, NJ: Princeton University Press.

Seeley, T. D. (1995). *The Wisdom of the Hive*. Cambridge, MA: Harvard University Press.

Seyfarth, R. M., & Cheney, D. L. (2003). Signalers and receivers in animal communication. *Annual Review of Psychology, 54*, 145–173.

Seyfarth, R. M., & Cheney, D. L. (2010). Production, use, and comprehension in animal vocalizations. *Brain and Language, 115*, 92–100.

Seyfarth, R. M., Cheney, D. L., Bergman, T. J., Fischer, J., Züberbuhler, K., & Hammerschmidt, K. (2010). The central importance of information in studies of communication. *Animal Behaviour, 80*, 3–8.

Seyfarth, R. M., Cheney, D. L., & Marler, P. (1980). Monkey responses to three different alarm calls: Evidence of predator classification and semantic communication. *Science, 210*, 801–803.

Shanks, D. R. (2010). Learning: From association to cognition. *Annual Review of Psychology, 61*, 273–301.

Shapiro, M. S., Siller, S., & Kacelnik, A. (2008). Simultaneous and sequential choice as a function of reward delay and magnitude: Normative, descriptive and process-based models tested in the European starling (*Sturnus vulgaris*). *Journal of Experimental Psychology: Animal Behavior Processes, 34*, 75–93.

Sherry, D. F. (2005). Do ideas about function help in the study of causation? *Animal Biology, 55*, 441–456.

Sherry, D. F. (2006). Neuroecology. *Annual Review of Psychology, 57*, 167–197.

Shettleworth, S. J. (1998). *Cognition, Evolution, and Behavior*. New York: Oxford University Press.

Shettleworth, S. J. (2010a). *Cognition, Evolution, and Behavior* (2nd ed.). New York: Oxford University Press.

Shettleworth, S. J. (2010b). Clever animals and killjoy explanations in comparative psychology. *Trends in Cognitive Sciences, 14*, 477–481.

Shettleworth, S. J., & Hampton, R. H. (1998). Adaptive specializations of spatial cognition in food storing birds? Approaches to testing a comparative hypothesis. In R. P. Balda, I. M. Pepperberg, & A. C. Kamil (Eds.), *Animal Cognition in Nature* (pp. 65–98). San Diego, CA: Academic Press.

Shettleworth, S. J., & Sutton, J. E. (2005). Multiple systems for spatial learning: Dead reckoning and beacon homing in rats. *Journal of Experimental Psychology: Animal Behavior Processes, 31*, 125–141.

Sheynikhovich, D., Chavarriaga, R., Strosslin, S., Arleo, A., & Gerstner, W. (2009). Is there a geometric module for spatial orientation? Insights from a rodent navigation model. *Psychological Review, 116*, 540–566.

Shumaker, R. W., Walkup, C. R., & Beck, B. B. (Eds.). (2011). *Animal Tool Behavior* (Revised and updated ed.). Baltimore, MD: Johns Hopkins University Press.

Silk, J. B. (1999). Male bonnet macaques use information about third-party rank relationships to recruit allies. *Animal Behaviour, 58*, 45–51.

Silk, J. B., & House, B. R. (2012). The phylogeny and ontogeny of prosocial behavior. In J. Vonk & T. Shackelford (Eds.), *Oxford Handbook of Comparative Evolutionary Psychology* (pp. 381–398). New York: Oxford University Press.

Silva, F. J., & Silva, K. M. (2006). Humans' folk physics is not enough to explain variations in their tool-using behavior. *Psychonomic Bulletin & Review, 13,* 689–693.

Silva, F. J., Silva, K. M., Cover, K. M., Leslie, A. L., & Rubalcaba, M. A. (2008). Humans' folk physics is sensitive to physical connection and contact between a tool and reward. *Behavioural Processes, 77,* 327–333.

Simon, H. A. (1962). The architecture of complexity. *Proceedings of the American Philosophical Society, 106,* 467–482.

Singer, R. A., Abroms, B. D., & Zentall, T. R. (2006). Formation of a simple cognitive map by rats. *International Journal of Comparative Psychology, 19,* 1–10.

Slotnick, B. (2001). Animal cognition and the rat olfactory system. *Trends in Cognitive Sciences, 5,* 216–222.

Smith, J. D., Chapman, W. P., & Redford, J. S. (2010). Stages of category learning in monkeys *(Macaca mulatta)* and humans *(Homo sapiens). Journal of Experimental Psychology: Animal Behavior Processes, 36,* 39–53.

Smith, J. D., Ashby, F. G., Berg, M. E., Murphy, R. A., Spiering, B., Cook, R. G., et al. (2011). Pigeons' categorization may be exclusively nonanalytic. *Psychonomic Bulletin & Review, 18,* 414–421.

Smith, J. D., Beran, M. J., Couchman, J. J., & Coutinho, M. V. C. (2008). The comparative study of metacognition: Sharper paradigms, safer inferences. *Psychonomic Bulletin & Review, 15,* 679–691.

Smith, J. D., Beran, M. J., Crossley, M. J., Boomer, J., & Ashby, F. G. (2010). Implicit and explicit category learning by macaques (*Macaca mulatta*) and humans (*Homo sapiens*). *Journal of Experimental Psychology: Animal Behavior Processes, 36,* 54–65.

Smith, J. D., Shields, W. E., Allendoerfer, K. R., & Washburn, D. A. (1998). Memory monitoring by animals and humans. *Journal of Experimental Psychology: General, 127,* 227–250.

Smith, J. D., Shields, W. E., & Washburn, D. A. (2003). The comparative psychology of uncertainty monitoring and metacognition. *Behavioral and Brain Sciences, 26,* 317–373.

Smith, J. D., & Washburn, D. A. (2005). Uncertainty monitoring and metacognition by animals. *Current Directions in Psychological Science, 14,* 19–24.

Sober, E. (2005). Comparative psychology meets evolutionary biology. Morgan's canon and cladistic parsimony. In L. Daston & G. Mitman (Eds.), *Thinking with animals: New perspectives on anthropomorphism* (pp. 85–99). New York: Columbia University Press.

Son, L. K., & Kornell, N. (2005). Meta-confidence judgments in rhesus macaques: Explicit vs. implicit mechanisms. In H. S. Terrace & J. Metcalfe (Eds.), *The Missing Link in Cognition: Origins of Self-Reflective Consciousness* (pp. 296–320). New York: Oxford University Press.

Spelke, E. S. (2000). Core knowledge. *American Psychologist*, *55*, 1233–1243.

Spelke, E. S., & Kinzler, K. D. (2007). Core knowledge. *Developmental Science*, *10*, 89–96.

Stephens, D. W., Brown, J. S., & Ydenberg, R. C. (Eds.). (2007). *Foraging*. Chicago, IL: University of Chicago Press.

Stephens, D. W., Kerr, B., & Fernández–Juricic, E. (2004). Impulsiveness without discounting: The ecological rationality hypothesis. *Proceedings of the Royal Society B*, *271*, 2459–2465.

Stevens, J. R., & Hauser, M. D. (2004). Why be nice? Psychological constraints on the evolution of cooperation. *Trends in Cognitive Sciences*, *8*, 60–65.

Stürzl, W., Cheung, A., Cheng, K., & Zeil, J. (2008). The information content of panoramic images I: The rotational errors and similarity of views in rectangular experimental arenas. *Journal of Experimental Psychology: Animal Behavior Processes*, *34*, 1–14.

Suddendorf, T., & Busby, J. (2005). Making decisions with the future in mind: Developmental and comparative identification of mental time travel. *Learning and Motivation*, *36*, 110–125.

Suddendorf, T., & Corballis, M. C. (1997). Mental time travel and the evolution of the human mind. *Genetic, Social, and General Psychology Monographs*, *123*, 133–167.

Suddendorf, T., & Corballis, M. C. (2008a). Episodic memory and mental time travel. In E. Dere, A. Easton, L. Nadel, & J. P. Huston (Eds.), *Handbook of Episodic Memory* (pp. 31–42). New York: Elsevier.

Suddendorf, T., & Corballis, M. C. (2008b). New evidence for animal foresight? *Animal Behaviour*, *25*, e1–e3.

Suddendorf, T., & Corballis, M. C. (2010). Behavioural evidence for mental time travel in nonhuman animals. *Behavioural Brain Research*, *215*, 292–298.

Suddendorf, T., Corballis, M. C., & Collier-Baker, E. (2009). How great is great ape foresight? *Animal Cognition*, *12*, 751–754.

Taylor, A. H., Hunt, G. R., Holzhaider, J. C., & Gray, R. D. (2007). Spontaneous metatool use by New Caledonian crows. *Current Biology*, *17*, 1504–1507.

Templeton, C. N., Greene, E., & Davis, K. (2005). Allometry of alarm calls: black-capped chickadees encode information about predator size. *Science*, *308*, 1934–1937.

Terrace, H. S. (2001). Chunking and serially organized behavior in pigeons, monkeys, and humans. In R. G. Cook (Ed.) *Avian Visual Cognition* [On-line]. Available: www.pigeon.psy.tufts.edu/avc/terrace/.

Terrace, H. S. (2006). The simultaneous chain: A new look at serially organized behavior. In E. A. Wasserman & T. R. Zentall (Eds.), *Comparative Cognition* (pp. 481–511). New York: Oxford University Press.

Thorndike, E. L. (1911/1970). *Animal Intelligence*. Darien, CT: Hafner Publishing Company.

Thornton, A., & McAuliffe, K. (2006). Teaching in wild meerkats. *Science, 313*, 227–229.

Thornton, A., & Raihani, N. J. (2010). Identifying teaching in wild animals. *Learning & Behavior, 38*, 297–309.

Thorpe, C. M., & Wilkie, D. M. (2006). Properties of time-place learning. In E. A. Wasserman & T. R. Zentall (Eds.), *Comparative Cognition: Experimental Explorations of Animal Intelligence* (pp. 229–245). New York: Oxford University Press.

Tinbergen, N. (1932/1972). On the orientation of the digger wasp *Philanthus triangulum* Fabr. I. (A. Rasa, Trans.). In N. Tinbergen (Ed.), *The Animal in Its World* (Vol. 1, pp. 103–127). Cambridge, MA: Harvard University Press.

Tinbergen, N. (1951). *The Study of Instinct*. Oxford, England: Oxford University Press.

Tinbergen, N. (1963). On aims and methods of ethology. *Zeitschrift fur Tierpsychologie, 20*, 410–433.

Todd, P. M., & Gigerenzer, G. (2007). Mechanisms of ecological rationality: Heuristics and environments that make us smart. In R. I. M. Dunbar & L. Barrett (Eds.), *The Oxford Handbook of Evolutionary Psychology* (pp. 197–210). Oxford, England: Oxford University Press.

Tolman, E. C. (1948). Cognitive maps in rats and men. *Psychological Review, 55*, 189–208.

Tolman, E. C., Ritchie, B. F., & Kalish, D. (1946). Studies in spatial learning. I. Orientation and the short-cut. *Journal of Experimental Psychology, 36*, 13–24.

Tomasello, M., & Call, J. (1997). *Primate Cognition*. New York: Oxford University Press.

Tomasello, M., Carpenter, M., Call, J., Behne, T., & Moll, H. (2005). Understanding and sharing intentions: The origins of cultural cognition. *The Behavioral and Brain Sciences, 28*, 675–735.

Tomasello, M., Davis-Dasilva, M., Camak, L., & Bard, K. (1987). Observational learning of tool-use by young chimpanzees. *Human Evolution, 2*, 175–183.

Treichler, F. R., Raghanti, M. A., & Van Tilburg, D. N. (2003). Linking of serially ordered lists by macaque monkeys (*Macaca mulatta*): List position influences. *Journal of Experimental Psychology: Animal Behavior Processes, 29*, 211–221.

Trivers, R. L. (1971). The evolution of reciprocal altruism. *The Quarterly Review of Biology, 46*, 35–57.

Tulving, E. (2005). Episodic memory and autonoesis: Uniquely human? In H. S. Terrace & J. Metcalfe (Eds.), *The Missing Link in Cognition: Origins of Self-Reflective Consciousness* (pp. 3–56). New York: Oxford University Press.

Udell, M. A. R., Dorey, N. R., & Wynne, C. D. L. (2010). What did domestication do to dogs? A new account of dogs' sensitivity to human actions. *Biological Reviews, 85*, 327–345.

van Heijningen, C. A. A., deVisser, J., Zuidema, W., & ten Cate, C. (2009). Simple rules can explain discrimination of putative syntactic structures by a songbird species. *Proceedings of the National Academy of Sciences USA, 106*, 20538–20543.

van Lawick-Goodall, J. (1971). Tool-using in primates and other vertebrates. *Advances in the Study of Behavior, 3*, 195–249.

von Bayern, A. M. P., Heathcote, R. J. P., Rutz, C., & Kacelnik, A. (2009). The role of experience in problem solving and innovative tool use in crows. *Current Biology, 19*, 1965–1968.

von Frisch, K. (1953). *The Dancing Bees* (D. Ilse, Trans.). New York: Harcourt Brace.

von Uexküll, J. (1934/1957). A stroll through the worlds of animals and men. In C. H. Schiller (Ed.), *Instinctive Behavior* (pp. 5–80). New York: International Universities Press.

Vonk, J., & Povinelli, D. J. (2006). Similarity and difference in the conceptual systems of primates: The unobservability hypothesis. In E. A. Wasserman & T. R. Zentall (Eds.), *Comparative Cognition* (pp. 363–387). New York: Oxford University Press.

Vonk, J., & Shackelford, T. (Eds.). (2012). *Oxford Handbook of Comparative Evolutionary Psychology.* New York: Oxford University Press.

Waldmann, M. R., Cheng, P. W., Hagmayer, Y., & Blaisdell, A. P. (2008). Causal learning in rats and humans: A minimal rational model. In N. Chater & M. Oaksford (Eds.), *The Probabilistic Mind: Prospects for Bayesian Cognitive Science* (pp. 453–484). Oxford, England: Oxford University Press.

Wall, P., Botly, L. C. P., Black, C. M., & Shettleworth, S. J. (2004). The geometric module in the rat: Independence of shape and feature learning in a food-finding task. *Learning & Behavior, 32*, 289–298.

Wang, R. F., & Brockmole, J. R. (2003). Human navigation in nested environments. *Journal of Experimental Psychology: Learning, Memory, and Cognition, 29*, 398–404.

Warneken, F., & Tomasello, M. (2009). Varieties of altruism in children and chimpanzees. *Trends in Cognitive Sciences, 13*, 397–402.

Wasserman, E. A., Hugart, J. A., & Kirkpatrick-Steger, K. (1995). Pigeons show same-different conceptualization after training with complex visual stimuli. *Journal of Experimental Psychology: Animal Behavior Processes, 21*, 248–252.

Wasserman, E. A., & Young, M. E. (2010). Same-different discrimination: The keel and backbone of thought and reasoning. *Journal of Experimental Psychology: Animal Behavior Processes, 36,* 3–22.

Wehner, R., & Srinivasan, M. V. (1981). Searching behaviour of desert ants, genus *Cataglyphis* (Formicidae, Hymenoptera). *Journal of Comparative Physiology A, 142,* 315–338.

Weir, A. A. S., Chappell, J., & Kacelnik, A. (2002). Shaping of hooks in New Caledonian crows. *Science, 297,* 981.

Weisberg, R. W. (2006). *Creativity.* Hoboken, NJ: John Wiley & Sons.

West-Eberhard, M. J. (2003). *Developmental Plasticity and Evolution.* New York: Oxford University Press.

Westneat, D. F., & Fox, C. W. (Eds.). (2010). *Evolutionary Behavioral Ecology.* New York: Oxford University Press.

Whishaw, I. Q., & Kolb, B. (Eds.). (2005). *The Behavior of the Laboratory Rat.* New York: Oxford University Press.

Whiten, A., Custance, D. M., Gomez, J-C., Teixidor, P., & Bard, K. A. (1996). Imitative learning of artificial fruit processing in children (*Homo sapiens*) and chimpanzees (*Pan troglodytes*). *Journal of Comparative Psychology, 110,* 3–14.

Whiten, A., Goodall, J., McGrew, W. C., Nishida, T., Reynolds, V., Sugiyama, Y., et al. (1999). Cultures in chimpanzees. *Nature, 399,* 682–685.

Whiten, A., Hinde, R. A., Stringer, C. B., & Laland, K. N. (2011). Culture evolves. *Philosophical Transactions of the Royal Society B, 366,* 938–948.

Whiten, A., McGuigan, N., Marshall-Pescini, S., & Hopper, L. M. (2009). Emulation, imitation, over-imitation and the scope of culture for child and chimpanzee. *Philosophical Transactions of the Royal Society B, 364,* 2417–2428.

Wiener, J., Shettleworth, S. J., Bingman, V. P., Cheng, K., Healy, S., Jacobs, L. F., et al. (2011). Animal navigation—A synthesis. In R. Menzel & J. Fischer (Eds.), *Animal Thinking: Contemporary Issues in Comparative Cognition* (pp. 51–76). Cambridge, MA: MIT Press.

Wilson, D. S., & Wilson, E. O. (2008). Evolution "for the good of the group." *American Scientist, 96,* 380–390.

Wimpenny, J. H., Weir, A. A. S., Clayton, L., Rutz, C., & Kacelnik, A. (2009). Cognitive processes associated with sequential tool use in New Caledonian crows. *PLoS One, 4,* e6471.

Wittlinger, M., Wehner, R., & Wolf, H. (2007). The desert ant odometer: A stride integrator that accounts for stride length and walking speed. *The Journal of Experimental Biology, 210,* 198–207.

Wright, A. A. (1991). A detection and decision process model of matching to sample. In M. L. Commons, J. A. Nevin, & M. C. Davison (Eds.), *Signal Detection: Mechanisms, Models, and Applications* (pp. 191–219). Hillsdale, NJ: Erlbaum.

Wright, A. A. (2006). Memory processing. In E. A. Wasserman & T. R. Zentall (Eds.), *Comparative Cognition: Experimental Explorations of Animal Intelligence* (pp. 164–185). New York: Oxford University Press.

Wright, A. A., Cook, R. G., & Rivera, J. J. (1988). Concept learning by pigeons: Matching-to-sample with trial-unique video picture stimuli. *Animal Learning & Behavior, 16*, 436–444.

Wright, A. A., Santiago, H. C., Sands, S. F., Kendrick, D. F., & Cook, R. G. (1985). Memory processing of serial lists by pigeons, monkeys, and people. *Science, 229*, 287–289.

Wynne, C. D. L. (2004). Fair refusal by capuchin monkeys. *Nature, 428*, 140.

Zentall, T. R. (2005). Selective and divided attention in animals. *Behavioural Processes, 69*, 1–15.

Zentall, T. R. (2010). Coding of stimuli by animals: Retrospection, prospection, episodic memory and future planning. *Learning and Motivation, 41*, 225–240.

Zentall, T. R., Clement, T. S., Bhatt, R. S., & Allen, J. (2001). Episodic-like memory in pigeons. *Psychonomic Bulletin & Review, 8*, 685–690.

Zentall, T. R., Sherburne, L. M., Roper, K. L., & Kraemer, P. J. (1996). Value transfer in a simultaneous discrimination appears to result from within-event Pavlovian conditioning. *Journal of Experimental Psychology: Animal Behavior Processes, 22*, 68–75.

Zhou, W. Y., & Crystal, J. D. (2009). Evidence for remembering when events occurred in a rodent model of episodic memory. *Proceedings of the National Academy of Sciences USA, 106*, 9525–9529.

Zuberbühler, K. (2008). Audience effects. *Current Biology, 18*, R189–R190.

Zuberbühler, K. (2009). Survivor signals: The biology and psychology of alarm calling. *Annual Review of Psychology, 40*, 227–232.

Zuberbühler, K., Cheney, D. L., & Seyfarth, R. M. (1999). Conceptual semantics in a nonhuman primate. *Journal of Comparative Psychology, 113*, 33–42.

CREDITS

....

1.2   Enard, W., & Pääbo, S. (2004). Comparative primate genomics. *Annual Review of Genomics and Human Genetics, 5*, 351–378. Copyright 2004 by Annual Reviews Inc.. Reproduced with permission.

2.2   Eacott, M.J., & Norman, G. (2004). Integrated memory for object, place, and context in rats: A possible model of episodic memory? *The Journal of Neuroscience, 24*, 1948–1953. Published by Society for Neuroscience.

2.3   Wright, A.A. (1991). A detection and decision process model of matching to sample. In M.L. Commons, J.A. Nevin, & M.C. Davison (eds.), *Signal Detection: Mechanisms, Models, and Applications*, 191–219: 10th Symposium on quantitative analysis of behavior. Reproduced with permission of Taylor & Francis Group LLC- Books.

2.3   Grant, D.S. (1976). Effect of sample presentation time on long–delay matching in pigeons. *Learning and Motivation, 7*, 580–590. Reproduced with permission of Academic Press.

2.4   From Wright, A.A., Santiago, H.C., Sands, S.F., Kendrick, D.F., & Cook, R.G. (1985). Memory processing of serial lists by pigeons, monkeys, and people. *Science, 229*, 287–289. Reproduced with permission of American Association for the Advancement of Science.

2.5   Hampton, R.R. (2001). Rhesus monkeys know when they remember. *Proceedings of the National Academy of Sciences, U.S.A., 98*, 5359–5362. Copyright © 2001 National Academy of Sciences, U.S.A. Adapted with permission.

2.7   Hanson, H.M. (1959). Effects of discrimination training on stimulus generalization. *Journal of Experimental Psychology, 58*, 321–324. Published by the American Psychological Association. Redrawn with permission.

2.8   Wasserman, E. A., Hugart, J.A., & Kirkpatrick-Steger, K. (1995). Pigeons show same-different conceptualization after training with complex stimuli. *Journal of Experimental Psychology: Animal Behavior Processes, 21*, 248–252. Copyright © 1995 by the American Psychological Association. Adapted with permission.

3.1a   Tinbergen, N. (1951). *The Study of Instinct.* By permission of Oxford University Press.

3.1c   Müller, M., & Wehner, R. (1988). Path integration in desert ants, *Cataglyphis fortis. Proceedings of the National Academy of Sciences, 85*, 5287–5290. Adapted with permission.

3.2   Stürzl, W., Cheung, A., Cheng, K., & Zeil, J. (2008). The information content of panoramic images I: The rotation errors and the similarity of views in rectangular experimental arenas. *Journal of Experimental Psychology: Animal Behavior Processes, 34*, 1–14. Copyright © 2008 by the American Psychological Association. Adapted with permission.

3.3   Tolman, E.C., Ritchie, B.F., & Kalish, D. (1946). Studies in spatial learning I. Orientation and the short cut. *Journal of Experimental Psychology, 34*, 13–24. Copyright © 1946 by the American Psychological Association. Adapted with permission.

3.4   Roberts, S. (1981). Isolation of an internal clock. *Journal of Experimental Psychology: Animal Behavior Processes, 7*, 242–268. Copyright © 1981 by the American Psychological Association. Adapted with permission.

3.5   Cantlon, J.F., & Brannon, E.M. (2006). Shared system for ordering small and large numbers in monkeys and humans. *Psychological Science, 17*, 401–406. Reproduced with permission of Blackwell Publishing Ltd.

3.6   Reprinted by permission from Macmillan Publishers Ltd.: Nature. Raby, C.R., Alexis, D.M., Dickinson, A., & Clayton, N.S., Planning for the future by western scrub–jays. Nature, 445, 919–921. Copyright © 2007. Reproduced with permission of Nature Publishing Group.

3.7   Redrawn from *Current Biology, 16*, Seed, A.M., Tebbich, S., Emery, N.J., Clayton, N.S., Investigation physical cognition in rooks, *Corvus frugilegus*, 697–701, Copyright © 2006, adapted with permission from Elsevier BV.

4.1   Redrawn from *Cognition, 56*, Gergely, G., Nádasdy, Z., Csibra, G., & Bíró, S., Taking the intentional stance at 12 months of age, 165–193, Copyright © 1995, with permission from Elsevier. Adapted with permission of Elsevier BV.

4.2   Redrawn from *Trends in Neurosciences, 18*, Povinelli, D.J., & Preuss, T.M., Theory of mind: Evolutionary history of a cognitive specialization, 418–424. Copyright © 1995. Reproduced with permission of Elsevier LTD.

4.3   From Jensen, K., Call, J., & Tomasello, M. (2007). Chimpanzees are rational maximizers in an ultimatum game. *Science, 318*, 107–109.

Redrawn with permission from the American Association for the Advancement of Science.

4.4 Whiten, A., Custance, D.M., Gomez, J.-C., Teixidor, P., & Bard, K.A. (1996). Imitative learning of artificial fruit processing in children (*Homo sapiens*) and chimpanzees (*Pan troglodytes*). *Journal of Comparative Psychology, 110*, 3–14. Copyright © 1996 by the American Psychological Association. Adapted with permission.

4.5 Seeley, Thomas, D.; *Honeybee Ecology*. Princeton University Press. Redrawn by permission of Princeton University Press.

NAME INDEX

....

Note: Illustrations and captions are indicated by *italic* page numbers.

SUBJECT INDEX

....

Note: Illustrations and captions are indicated by *italic* page numbers.